The Secret Trails

by Charles G. D. Roberts

CONTENTS

THE SECRET TRAILS

The Black Boar of Lonesome Water

I

The population of Lonesome Water--some fourscore families in all--acknowledged one sole fly in the ointment of its self-satisfaction. Slowly, reluctantly, it had been brought to confess that the breed of its pigs was not the best on earth. They were small, wiry pigs, over-leisurely of growth, great feeders, yet hard to fatten; and in the end they brought but an inferior price in the far-off market town by the sea, to which their frozen, stiff-legged carcases were hauled on sleds over the winter's snow. It was decided by the village council that the breed must be severely improved.

They were a peculiar people, the dwellers about the remote and lovely shores of Lonesome Water. They were the descendants of a company of Welsh sectarians who, having invented a little creed of their own which was the sole repository of truth and righteousness, had emigrated to escape the contamination of their neighbours. They had come to Canada because Canada was not crowded; and they had chosen the lovely valley of Lonesome Water, not for its loveliness, but for its lonesomeness and its fertility, and for the fact that it was surrounded by tracts of barren land which might keep off the defilements of the world. Here they devoted themselves to farming and to the contemplation of their own superiority; and having a national appreciation of the value of a half-penny, they prospered.

As may easily be understood, it was no small thing for the people of Lonesome Water to be forced, by the unanswerable logic of the market price, to acknowledge that their pigs were inferior to the pigs of the ungodly. Of course, there were many in the Settlement who refused flatly to believe that this could be so. Providence could not be so short-sighted as to permit it. But the majority faced the truth with solemn resolution. And Morgan Fluellyn, the hog reeve of Lonesome Water, was sent to K-ville, to interview the secretary of the provincial agricultural society, and to purchase--if it could be done at a bargain--some pigs of a pedigree worthy the end in view.

In the eyes of Morgan Fluellyn--small, deep-set, choleric eyes--the town of

K-ville, with its almost two thousand inhabitants, its busy picture show, its three pubs, its cheerful, friendly girls, who adorned their hats with lavish flowers and feathers, was a place upon which the fires of an outraged heaven might some day fall. He had no mind to be caught in K-ville at the moment of this merited catastrophe. He lost no time in putting through his business.

When he found the secretary, and learned the price of pedigree pigs, his indignation nearly choked him. With righteous sternness he denounced the secretary, the society, and the Government, and stalked from the office. But an hour in the air brought him to a clearer understanding, and his ambitions on behalf of his community revived. Lonesome Water had the truth. She had a monopoly of the virtues. She should also have pigs that would command these outrageous prices. Why should the ungodly triumph?

And they did not--at least, not altogether. Morgan Fluellyn was allowed to achieve a bargain. The mollified secretary consented to sell him, at a reduced figure, a big black Berkshire boar, of unimpeachable breeding, but small success in the show-pen, and in temper not to be relied on. The great boar had a steel ring through his snout, and Fluellyn set out with him proudly. Fluellyn was delighted with his prize, but it appeared that his prize was not equally delighted with Fluellyn. In fact, the great grunting beast was surly and cantankerous from the first. He would look at his purchaser with a malign cunning in his eyes, and sometimes make a slash at his leg with gnashing jaws. But Fluellyn was by no means lacking in the valour and pugnacity of his race, and his patience was of the shortest. By means of that rope through his captive's snout, he had an advantage which he knew how to make the most of. The fringe of fiery whisker, which haloed his red, clean-shaven cheeks and chin like a ruff, fairly curled with wrath at the beast's presumption, and he administered such discipline with his cudgel as he felt sure would not soon be forgotten.

After this, for mile upon mile of the lonely backwoods trail, there was peace, and even an apparent unanimity of purpose, between Fluellyn and his sullenly grunting charge. But the great black boar was not really subdued. He was merely biding his time. And because he bided it cunningly, his time came.

The trail was bad, the going hard, for there was no unnecessary travel either way between Lonesome Water and her neighbour settlements. Fluellyn was tired. It was getting along in the afternoon. He sat down on a log which lay invitingly by the side of the trail. From the bag of feed which he carried on his back, he poured out a goodly allowance for the black boar, being not unwilling to keep the brute amiable. Then he seated himself on the log, in the caressing spring sunshine, and pulled out his pipe. For Fluellyn smoked. It was his one concession to human weakness, and it had almost lost him his election as hog-reeve. Nevertheless, he smoked. The air was bland, and he, too, became almost bland. His choleric eyes grew visionary. He forgot to distrust the black boar.

The perfidious beast devoured its feed with noisy enthusiasm, at the same time watching Fluellyn out of the corner of its wicked little eye. When the feed was finished, it flashed about without a ghost of a warning and charged full upon Fluellyn.

Behind the log on which Fluellyn sat the ground fell away almost perpendicularly, perhaps, twelve or fifteen feet, to the edge of a foaming brown trout-brook fringed with alders. As the boar charged, Fluellyn sprang to his feet. At the same time he tried to spring backwards. His heels failed to clear the log; and in this his luck was with him, for the boar this time meant murder. He plunged headlong, with a yell of indignation, over the steep. And the animal, checking itself at the brink, glared down upon him savagely, gnashing its tusks.

Fluellyn was quite seriously damaged by his fall. His head and forehead were badly cut, so that his face was bathed in blood and dirt, through which his eyes glared upward no less fiercely than those of his adversary. His left arm was broken and stabbing at him with keen anguish, but he was too enraged to notice his hurts, and if it had been suggested to him that his fall had saved his life, he would have blown up with fury. He flew at the face of the steep like a wild-cat, struggling to scramble up it and get at the foe. But in this purpose, luckily for him, he was foiled by his broken arm. The boar, too, though eager to follow up his triumph, durst not venture the descent.

For some minutes, therefore, the antagonists faced each other, the boar leaning over as far as he could, with vicious squeals and grunts and slaverings and gnashings, while the indomitable Fluellyn, with language which he had never guessed himself capable of, and which would have caused his instant expulsion from Lonesome Water, defied and reviled him, and strove to claw up to him. At last the boar, who, being the victor, could best afford it, grew tired of the game. Tossing his armed snout in the air, he drew back from the brink and trotted off into the fir-woods on the other side of the trail. Delighted with his first taste of freedom, he kept on for some miles without a halt, till at last he came to a pond full of lily leaves, with soft black mud about its edges. Here he lay down and wallowed till his wrath cooled. Then he stretched himself in the grass and went to sleep.

As for Fluellyn, his wrath had no excuse for cooling, for the anguish of his hurts at last diverted his attention from it, more or less. He stumbled on down the stream till he reached a spot where he could get up the bank. By this time he was feeling faint, and his angry eyes were half blinded with the blood which he kept wiping from them with his sleeve. Nevertheless, he returned to the scene of his overthrow, and from that point, without a thought of prudence, took up the trail of the boar through the fir thickets. But he was no expert in woodcraft at the best of times, and the trail soon eluded him. Forced at last to confess himself worsted for the moment, he made his way back to the log, snatched up the bag of feed, that his enemy might not return and enjoy it, and with dogged resolution set his face once more toward Lonesome Water.

When he arrived there, he was babbling in a fever. His appearance was a scandal, and his language cleared the village street. There were many who held that he had gone astray under the wicked influence of K-ville--which was no more than they had always said would happen to a man who smoked tobacco. But the majority were for not condemning him when he was unable to defend himself. For three weeks he lay helpless. And by the time he was well enough to tell his story, which was convincing to all but the sternest of his censors, the black boar had wandered so far into the wilderness that he was safe from pursuit. There were no woodsmen in Lonesome Water cunning enough to follow up his obscure and devious trail.

II

In spite of the allurements of the lily pool, the black boar forsook it after a couple of blissful days' wallowing. The wanderlust, choked back for generations, had awakened in his veins. He pushed on, not caring in what direction, for perhaps a fortnight. Though food was everywhere abundant, he had always to work for it, so he grew lean and hard and swift. The memory of a thousand years of servitude slipped from him, as it were, in a night, and at the touch of the wilderness many of the instincts and aptitudes of a wild thing sprang up in him. Only the instinct of concealment, of stealth, was lacking to this new equipment of his. He feared nothing, and he hunted nothing more elusive than lily-roots; so he took no care to disguise his movements.

At first, because of the noise he made, the forest seemed to him to be empty of all living things but birds. Then one day, as he lay basking in the sun, he saw a wild-cat pounce upon a rabbit. At first he stared curiously. But when he saw the wild-cat feasting on her prey, he decided that he wanted the banquet for himself. As he burst through the bushes, the great cat stared for an instant in utter amazement, never having seen or dreamed of such an apparition. Then, her eyes like moons, her six-inch bob-tail fluffed to a bottle-brush, and every hair stiffly on end, she bounced into the nearest tree. There in a crotch she crouched, spitting and yowling, while her enemy tranquilly devoured the rabbit. The tit-bit was not altogether to his taste, but he chose to eat it rather than let the great cat have it. And, after all, it was something of a change from roots and fungi.

Having thus discovered that rabbits were more or less edible, the black boar thenceforward chased them whenever they crossed his path. He never came anywhere near the catching of them, but, in spite of that, he was not discouraged. Some day, perhaps, he would meet a rabbit that could not run so fast as the others.

Fond as the boar was of wallowing in the cool mud of the lily ponds, he was, in reality, a stickler for personal cleanliness. When the mud was dry, he would roll in the moss, and scratch himself till it was all rubbed off, leaving his black bristles in perfect condition. His habits were as dainty as a cat's, and his bed of dead leaves, in the heart of some dense thicket, was always kept dry and fastidiously clean.

One day, as he lay asleep in one of these shadowy lairs, a bear came by, moving noiselessly in the hope of surprising a rabbit or a brooding partridge. A breath of air brought to the great prowler's nostrils a scent which seemed to him strongly out of place there in the depths of the forest. He stopped, lifted his muzzle, and sniffed critically. Yes, that smell was unquestionably pig. Once he had captured a fat young pig on the outskirts of a settler's farm, and his jaws watered at the delicious remembrance.

Crouching low, he crept up toward the thicket, led by his discriminating nose. His huge paws made no more sound than the gliding of a shadow. Peering in through the tangle of twigs and leafage, he was able to make out some black creature asleep. He paused suspiciously. The pig of his remembrance was white and much smaller than the animal he saw before him. Still, his nose assured him that this was pig all right. His appetite hushed his prudence, and, crashing into the thicket, he hurled himself upon the slumbering form.

And then a strange thing--a most disconcerting thing--happened to him. That slumbering form heaved up beneath him, grunting, and shot out between his hind legs with a violence which pitched him forward on his nose. Before he could recover himself, it wheeled about, looking many times larger than he had imagined it to be, and charged upon him with an ear-splitting squeal of rage. The shock bowled him clean over, so that he rolled out of the thicket, and at the same time he got a tearing slash down his flank. Startled quite out of his customary pugnacious courage, he bawled like a yearling cub, scrambled to his feet, and took to flight ignominiously. But the unknown fury behind him could run as fast as he, and it clung to his heels, squealing horribly and rooting at his rump with murderous tusks. In a panic he clawed his way up the nearest tree.

Finding himself no longer pursued, he turned and stared down from among the branches. He saw that his victorious adversary was indeed a pig, but such a pig! He felt himself most treacherously ill-used--betrayed, in fact. It was out of all fitness that a pig should be so big, so black, and so abrupt in manners. Had he dared to put the matter again to the test, he might have avenged his defeat, for he was much the heavier of the two, and immeasurably the better armed for battle. But he had no stomach to face that squealing fury again. He crawled on up to a convenient crotch, and lay there licking his scars and whimpering softly to himself, his appetite for pork entirely spoiled.

The boar, after ramping about beneath the tree for a matter of perhaps a half hour, at last trotted off in disgust, confirmed in his arrogance. This easy victory over so large and formidable a foe convinced him, had he needed any convincing, that he was lord of the wilderness. Had he chanced, about that time, to meet another bear, of sturdier resolution than the first, he would have had a rude disillusionment.

As it was, however, no later than the following day he had an adventure which jarred his complacence. It taught him not exactly prudence, but, at least, a certain measure of circumspection, which was afterwards to profit him. It was just on the edge of evening, when the wilderness world was growing vague with violet shadows, and new, delicate scents were breathing from leaf and bush at the touch of the dew, that the confident wanderer caught sight of a little black-and-white striped animal. It was hardly as large as a rabbit. It was not the colour of a rabbit. It had by no means the watchful, timorous air of a rabbit. As a matter of fact, it was a skunk; but his far-off ancestors had neglected to hand down to him any informatory instinct about skunks. He jumped to the conclusion that it was a rabbit, all the same-- perhaps the fat, slow rabbit which he had been hoping to come across. He hurled himself upon it with his utmost dash, determined that this time the elusive little beast should not escape him.

And it didn't. In fact, it hardly tried to. When he was within a few feet of it, it jerked its long tail into the air, and at the same time something dreadful and incomprehensible struck him in the face. It struck him in the eyes, the nose, the mouth, all at the same time. It scalded him, it blinded him, it suffocated him, it sickened him. He tried to stop himself, but he was too late. His impetus carried him on so that he trod down and killed the little animal without being aware of it.

In fact, he paid no attention whatever to his victory. All he cared about, for the moment, was breath. His outraged lungs had shut up tight to keep out the intolerable invader. At last they opened, with a hoarse gasp of protest at being forced to. Having regained his breath, such as it was, he wanted to see. But his eyes were closed with a burning, clinging, oily stuff, which also clung foully in his nostrils and in his mouth. He strove clumsily to rub them clear with his fore-hooves, and, failing in this, he flung himself on his back with head outstretched and rolled frantically in the moss. Achieving thus a measure of vision out of one inflamed and blurred eye, he caught sight of a marshy pool gleaming through the trees. Gasping, coughing, blundering into tree and bush as he went, he rushed to the water's edge and plunged his outraged features as deep as he could into the cool slime. There he rooted and champed and wallowed till the torment grew less intolerable to all his senses, and his lungs once more performed their office without a spasm.

But still that deadly taint clung nauseatingly to his nostrils and his palate; and at last, quite beside himself with the torment, he emerged from the water and started on a mad gallop through the woods, trying to run away from it. He ran till he sank exhausted and fell into a heavy sleep. When he woke up, there was the smell still with him, and for days he could scarcely eat for the loathing of it.

Gradually, however, the clean air and the deodorizing forest scents made him once more tolerable to himself. But the lesson was not forgotten. When, one bright and wind-swept morning, he came face to face with a young porcupine, he stopped politely. The porcupine also stopped and slowly erected its quills till its size was almost doubled. The boar was much surprised. This sudden enlargement, indeed, was so incomprehensible that it angered him. The strange absence of fear in the nonchalant little creature also angered him. He was inclined to rush upon it at once and chew it up. But the fact that its colour was more or less black-and-white gave him a painful reminder of his late experience. Perhaps this was another of those slow rabbits! He checked himself and sniffed suspiciously. The stranger, with a little grumbling squeak, came straight at him--not swiftly, or, indeed, angrily, but with a confident deliberation that was most upsetting. The boar was big enough to have stamped the porcupine's life out with one stroke of his hoof. But instead of standing up to his tiny challenger, he turned tail and bolted off squealing through the undergrowth as if nothing less than a troop of lions were after him.

III

The course of the black boar's wanderings brought him out at last upon the desolate northern shores of Lonesome Water. At night he could sometimes see, miles away across the lake, a gleam of the discreet lights of the Settlement--perhaps, indeed, from the windows of Morgan Fluellyn himself, whose cottage was close down on the waterside. This northern shore, being mostly swamp and barren, was entirely ignored by the dwellers in Lonesome

Water Settlement, who were satisfied with their own fertile fields, and not of an inquiring temperament. But it offered the black boar just the retreat he was now in search of. Tired of wandering, he found himself a lair in a dense and well-drained thicket near the bank of a lilied stream which here wound slowly through reeds and willows to the lake.

Here, with food abundant, and never skunk or smell of skunk to challenge his content, he wallowed and rooted the gold-and-green summer away and found life good. He was not troubled by forebodings of the winter, because he had never known anything of winter beyond the warmth of a well-provided pen.

One dreamy and windless afternoon in late September, when a delicate bluish haze lay over the yellowing landscape, a birch canoe was pushed in among the reeds, and a woodsman in grey homespun stepped ashore. He was gaunt and rugged of feature, with quiet, keen, humorous eyes, and he moved in his soft hide "larrigans" as lightly as a cat. He knew of a little ice-cold spring in this neighbourhood not far from the river bank, and he never passed the spot without stopping to drink deep at its preternaturally crystal flow.

He had not gone more than fifty yards up the shore when his eye was caught by a most unusual trail. He stopped to examine it. As he did so, a sudden crash in the bushes made him turn his head sharply. A massive black shape, unlike anything he had ever seen before, was charging down upon him. Whatever it was--and he remembered a picture he had once seen of a wild boar charging a party of hunters--he knew it meant mischief of the worst kind. And he had left his gun in the canoe. Under the circumstances, he was not too proud to run. He ran well, which was lucky for him. As he swung up his long legs into the branches, the black boar reared himself against the trunk, gnashing his tusks and squealing furiously. The man, from his safe perch, looked down upon him thoughtfully for perhaps a whole minute.

"Well, I'll be durned!" he ejaculated at last, getting out his pipe and slowly filling it. "Ef 'tain't Fluellyn's pig! To think Jo Peddler 'ld ever have to run from a pig!"

For perhaps a half hour Peddler sat there and smoked contentedly enough, with the patience which the wilderness teaches to all its children. He expected his gaoler to go away and let him make a dash for the canoe. But presently he concluded that the boar had no intention of going away. If so, it was time to do something if he wanted to get across the lake before dark.

He cleaned the ashes out of his pipe and saved them carefully. Then he refilled the pipe very loosely and smoked it violently half through, which yielded him another collection of pungent ash. He repeated the process several times, till he judged he had enough of the mixture--ash and dry, powdered tobacco. Then, grinning, he let himself down till he was barely out of reach, and began to tease and taunt his gaoler till the surly beast was beside itself with rage, snorting and squealing and rearing itself against the trunk in its efforts to get at him. At length, with infinite pains and precision, he sifted the biting mixture into his adversary's eyes and wide, snorting nostrils. By great good luck he managed to hit the mark exactly. How he wished the stuff had been pepper!

At the result he nearly fell out of the tree with ecstasy. The boar's squeal was cut short by a paroxysm of choking and coughing. The great animal nearly fell over backwards. Then, remembering his ancient experience with the skunk, he rushed blindly for the water, his eyes, for the most part, screwed up tight, so that he crashed straight through everything that stood in his path. Peddler dropped from his refuge and ran for his canoe, laughing delightedly as he ran. What little grudge he owed the animal for his temporary imprisonment, he felt to have been amply repaid, and he was glad he had not yielded to his first impulse and emptied the hot coals from his pipe into its nostrils.

"I'll be givin' yer compliments to Fluellyn," he shouted, as he paddled away, "an' likely he'll be over to call on ye afore long!"

IV

Jo Peddler had small love for the peculiar community of Lonesome Water. He never visited it except under the necessity of buying supplies for his camp. He used to swear that its very molasses was sour, that its tea was so self-righteous that it puckered his mouth. He never slept under one of its roofs, choosing, rather, to pitch his tent in the patch of dishevelled common on the outskirts of the village.

On the morning after his interview with the black boar, he was making his purchases at the village grocery--a "general" shop which sold also hardware, dry goods, and patent medicines, and gave a sort of disapproving harbourage to the worldly postoffice--when Morgan Fluellyn dropped in, nodded non-committally, and sat down on a keg of nails. To Peddler the bad-tempered little Welshman was less obnoxious than most of his fellow-villagers, both because he was so far human as to smoke tobacco, and because his reputation and self-satisfaction had been damaged by the episode of the pedigree boar. There was little tenderness toward damaged goods, or anything else, in Lonesome Water, so the woodsman felt almost friendly toward Fluellyn.

"What'll ye be givin' me," he inquired, proffering his plug of choice tobacco, "ef I git yer pig back fer ye?"

Fluellyn so far forgot himself as to spring eagerly to his feet. His fringe of red whisker fairly curled forward to meet Peddler's suggestion. If he could restore the precious animal to the community, his prestige would be re-established. Moreover, his own sore shaken self-esteem would lift its head and flourish once again.

"I'd pay ye right well, Jo Peddler," he declared, forgetting his native prudence in a bargain. "Can ye do it, man?"

"I can that," replied Peddler. And the storekeeper, with a half-filled kerosene tin in his hand, came forward to listen.

"I'm a poor man," went on Fluellyn, recollecting himself with a jerk and sitting down again on the nail keg. "I'm a poor man, as Mr. Perley here'll tell ye, an' I've already had to pay for the pig out o' my own pocket. An' it's cost me a fearful sum for the doctor. But I've said I want the pig back, and I'd pay ye well. An' I won't go back on my word. What'll ye take now?"

"I know ye've been playing in hard luck, Fluellyn," said the woodsman genially, "an' I ain't a-drivin' no bargain. I know what that there pig cost ye down to K-ville. But he ain't no manner o' use to me. He ain't what ye'd call a household pet, as ye'll agree. I'll find him and ketch him an' deliver him to ye, sound in wind an' limb, down here at the landin', if ye'll promise to pay me four pound for my trouble when the job's rightly done. An' Mr. Perley here's my witness."

Fluellyn drew a sigh of relief. He thought the woodsman a fool to be so moderate, but he was not without an inkling of the truth that this moderation was due to generosity and kindness rather than to folly. To his amazement, he felt a prompting to be generous himself.

"Tell ye what I'll do," said he, springing up again and grasping Peddler's hand. "If ye'll take me along an' let me help ye fix him, I'll make it five pound instead o' four. He done me bad, an' I'd like to git square."

"All right," said Peddler, with an understanding grin.

On the following morning Peddler and Fluellyn set out for the north shore of the lake. They went in a roomy row-boat, and they carried with them an assortment of ropes and straps. They started very early, just on the edge of dawn; for even here, in Lonesome Water, were to be found certain spirits so imperfectly regenerate as to be not above curiosity, not above a worldly itching to see the outcome of the venture; and Peddler would have no marplots about to risk the upsetting of his plans.

When they set out, the unruffled surface of the lake lay gleaming in vast, irregular breadths and patches of polished steel-grey and ethereal ice-blue and miraculous violet-silver, so beautiful that Peddler almost shrank from breaking the charmed stillness with his oars, and even Fluellyn felt strange stirrings within him of a long-atrophied sense of beauty. The village of Lonesome Water slumbered heavily, with windows and hearts alike close shut.

The sun was high in the hot blue when the boat, with stealthy oars, crept in among the reeds and made a noiseless landing.

"If ye stir a foot outside the boat till I call to ye, Fluellyn, the bargain's off, an' ye kin ketch the pig yerself," admonished Peddler in a whisper, as he stole up the shore with a coil of ropes over his left arm and a steel-shod canoe-pole in his right hand.

He kept a wary eye on the thicket which he judged to be the black boar's lair, until he was close to the foot of the tree in which he had previously taken refuge. Then he coughed loudly, announcing his presence. But there was no response from the thicket.

"Come out o' that, ye black divil, an' I'll truss ye up like a bale o' hay!" he shouted.

As if this inducement was something quite irresistible, came a sudden crashing, not in the thicket he was watching, but in the bushes directly behind him, not a dozen paces away. Without stopping to look round, he dropped his pole and jumped for the tree.

"Bad luck to ye," he growled, as he gained his perch just in time, "taking a feller by surprise that way!"

As the beast squealed and ramped below, Peddler leaned down from his perch and flicked it smartly with one of his lengths of rope, till it was jumping up and down and almost bursting with rage. Then, securing the rope to a stout branch, he made a slip-knot in the end of it and tried to throw it over the boar's fore-leg. After half a dozen failures, he made a lucky cast and instantly drew the noose tight.

Instead of being daunted at this, the boar again rushed furiously at the tree, rearing himself against it in a repetition of his former tactics. This gave Peddler just the chance he wanted.

"That's where ye've made the mistake, now," said he sympathetically, and dropped another noose well over the beast's snout, beyond the tusks. As he drew it tight, he took up the slack of both ropes in a deft hitch over the branch; and the boar found itself strung up against the trunk, dancing frantically on its hind legs, and no longer able even to squeal effectively.

"Maybe ye'll be a mite more civil now," mocked Peddler, and dropped lightly from his branch to the ground.

In half a minute he had whipped the frantic boar's two front legs together, also its two hind legs, run a sliding rope from the one pair to the other, and muzzled the formidable jaws more securely with a leather skate-strap. Then he freed the ropes from above and lowered his prisoner carefully to the ground, where it struggled madly till he drew its fore legs and hind legs close together by means of the sliding rope. Thus trussed up, it seemed at last to realize its defeat, and lay still upon its side, breathing heavily, which, indeed, was about the only form of activity left to it. Peddler stood off and surveyed his captive benignantly as he filled his pipe. "Fluellyn," he called, "ye kin come now an' have a talk with yer pig!"

With a bound, Fluellyn came up the bank, burning to avenge his humiliations, his cheeks glowing in their halo of crisp red whisker. But at sight of the great boar lying trussed up so ignobly his face fell.

"Why didn't ye let me have a hand in the job?" he demanded resentfully.

"Sorry," said Peddler, "but it couldn't be done nohow. Ye'd hev spiled the whole game, an' like as not got yer gizzard ripped. Now ye've got him, I allow ye hain't got nawthin' to grumble at." And he waited curiously to see what the little Welshman would do to relieve his feelings.

But Fluellyn, with all his faults, was not the man to kick a fallen foe. For some moments he eyed the helpless black monster with so sinister a gaze that Peddler thought he was devising some cruel vengeance, and made ready to interfere, if necessary. But all Fluellyn did, in the end, was to go over and seat himself comfortably on the great beast's panting flank and proceed to fill his pipe.

"It's goin' to be a hefty job a-gettin' him into the boat," said he at length, sternly repressing the note of exultation that would creep into his voice.

The Dog that saved the Bridge

I

The old canal lay dreaming under the autumn sun, tranquil between its green banks and its two rows of stiffly-rimmed bordering poplars. Once a busy highway for barges, it was now little more than a great drainage ditch, with swallow and dragon-flies darting and flashing over its seldom ruffled surface. Scattered here and there over the fat, green meadows beyond its containing dykes, fat cows lay lazily chewing the cud.

It was a scene of unmarred peace. To the cows nothing could have seemed more impregnable than their security. Off south-westward and southward, to be sure, the horizon was columned, decoratively but ominously, by pillars of dense smoke, sharp against the turquoise sky. But such phenomena, however novel, failed to stir the cows to even the mildest curiosity. The spacious summer air, however, was entertaining a strange riot of noises. It thumped and throbbed and thundered. It seemed to be ripped across from time to time with a dry, leisurely sound of tearing. Again, it would be suddenly shattered with enormous earth-shaking crashes. But all this foolish tumult was in the distance, and it gave the cows not the slightest concern. It had not interfered with the excellent quality of the pasturage; it had not disturbed the regularity of milking-time.

Strategically considered, the lazy old canal led from nowhere to nowhere, and the low levels through which it ran were aside from the track of the fighting. The peasant folk on their little farms still went about their business, but very quietly and with lowered voices, as if hoping thus to avoid the eye of Fate.

Along the grass-grown towpath, marching in half-sections, came a tiny detachment of long-coated Belgian riflemen with a machine-gun. The deadly little weapon, on its two-wheeled toy carriage, was drawn by a pair of sturdy, brindled dogs--mongrels, evidently, showing a dash of bull and a dash of retriever in their make-up. They were not as large as the dogs usually employed by the Belgians in this kind of service, but they were strong, and keen on their job. Digging their strong toes into the turf, they threw their weight valiantly into the straps, and pressed on, with tongues hanging out and what looked like a cordial grin on their panting jaws. They seemed desperately afraid of being left behind by their quick-marching comrades.

The little band kept well under the trees as they went, lest some far-scouting aeroplane should catch sight of them. In the south-eastern sky, presently, an aeroplane--a Taube--did appear; but it was so distant that the young lieutenant in command of the detachment, after examining it carefully with his field-glasses, concluded that it was little likely to detect his dark line moving under the trees. The Taube, that execrated dove of death, was spying over the Belgian trenches, and doubtless daring a hot fire from the Belgian rifles. Once it made a wide sweep north-westward, rapidly growing larger, and the little band under the trees lay down, hiding themselves and the gun behind the dyke. Then its flight swerved back over the Belgian lines, and the commander, lowering his glasses with a deep breath of relief, gave the order to march. Two minutes later, around the questing aeroplane appeared a succession of sudden fleecy puffs of smoke, looking soft and harmless as cotton-wool. One of these came just before the nose of the aeroplane. Next moment the machine gave a great swooping dive, righted itself, dived again, and dropped like a stone.

"Thank God for that!" muttered the young lieutenant, and his men cheered grimly under their breath.

Three minutes later the detachment came to an old stone bridge. Here it halted. The men began hastily entrenching themselves where they could best command the approaches on the other side. The machine-gun, lifted from its little carriage, was placed cunningly behind a screen of reeds. The two dogs, panting, lay down in their harness under a thick bush. In an amazingly brief time the whole party was so hidden that no one approaching from the other side of the canal could have guessed there was anything more formidable in the neighbourhood than the ruminating cows.

The neglected, almost forgotten, old bridge had suddenly leapt into importance. Reinforcements for the sore-pressed division to the south-east were being sent around by the north of the canal, and were to cross by the bridge. The detachment had been sent to guard the bridge at all costs from any wide-roving patrols of Uhlans who might take it into their heads to blow it up. In war it is a pretty safe principle to blow up any bridge if you are quite sure you won't be wanting it yourself. The fact that the other side has spared it is enough to damn it off-hand.

The tumult of the far-off gunfire was so unremitting that the ears of the bridge-guard gradually came to accept it as a mere background, against which small, insignificant sounds, if sudden and unexpected, became strangely conspicuous. The crowing of a cock in the farmyard a few fields off, the sharp cry of a moorhen, the spasmodic gabbling of a flock of fat ducks in the canal-- these small noises were almost as clearly differentiated as if heard in a stark silence.

For perhaps an hour the detachment had lain concealed, when those ominous pillars of smoke against the sky were joined suddenly by swarms of the little white puffs of cotton-wool, and the confused noises redoubled in violence. The battle was swaying nearer and spreading around a swiftly widening arc of the low horizon. Then another aeroplane--another bird-like Taube--came in view, darting up from a little south of west. The young lieutenant, in his hiding-place beside the bridge-head clapped his glasses anxiously to his eyes. Yes, the deadly flier was heading straight for this position. Evidently the Germans knew of that out-of-the-way bridge, and in their eyes also, for some reason, it had suddenly acquired importance. The Taube was coming to see in what force it was held.

"Spies again!" he grunted savagely, turning to explain to his men.

Flying at a height of only five or six hundred metres, the Taube flew straight over them. There was no longer any use in attempting concealment. The riflemen opened fire upon it furiously as soon as it came within range. It was hit several times; but the Taube is a steel machine, well protected from below, and neither the pilot nor any vital part of the mechanism was damaged. It made haste, however, to climb and swerve away from so hot a neighbourhood. But first, as a message of defiance, it dropped a bomb. The bomb fell sixty or seventy yards away from the bridge back in the meadow, among a group of cows. The explosion killed one cow and wounded several. The survivors, thus rudely shocked out of their indifference, stamped off down the field, tails in air and bellowing frantically.

"That cooks our goose," snapped one of the riflemen concisely.

"Their shells'll be dead on to us in ten minutes' time," growled another. And all cursed soberly.

"I don't think so," said the young lieutenant, after a moment's hesitation. "They want the bridge, so they won't shell it. But you'll see they'll be on to us shortly with their mitrailleuse and half a battalion or so, enough to eat us up. We've got to get word back quick to the General for reinforcements, or the game's up."

"I'll go, my lieutenant," said Jean Ferr 闹 l, an eager, dark Walloon, springing to his feet.

The lieutenant did not answer for some moments. He was examining through his glasses a number of mounted figures, scattering over the plains to the rear in groups of two and three. Yes, they were Uhlans unquestionably. The line of combat was shifting eastward.

"No," said he, "you can't go, Jean. You'd never get through. The Bosches are all over the place back there now. And you wouldn't be in time, even if you did get through. I'll send one of the dogs."

He tore a leaf out of his note-book and began scribbling.

"Better send both dogs, my lieutenant," said Jan Steen, the big, broad-built Fleming who had charge of the machine-gun, unharnessing the dogs as he spoke. "Leo's the cleverest, and he'll carry the message right; but he won't have his heart in the job unless you let Dirck go along with him. They're like twins. Moreover, the two together wouldn't excite suspicion like one alone. One alone the Bosches would take for a messenger dog, sure, but two racing over the grass might seem to be just playing."

"Bon!" said the young lieutenant. "Two strings to our bow."

He hurriedly made a duplicate of his dispatch. The papers were folded small and tied under the dogs' collars. Big Jan spoke a few words crisply and decisively in Flemish to Leo, who watched his lips eagerly and wagged his tail as if to show he understood. Then he spoke similarly, but with more emphasis and reiteration, to Dirck, at the same time waving his arm toward the distant group of roofs from which the detachment had come. Dirck looked anxiously at him and whined, and then glanced inquiringly at Leo, to see if he understood what was required of them. He was almost furiously willing, but not so quick to catch an idea as his more lively yoke-fellow. Big Jan repeated his injunctions yet again, with unhurried patience, while his leader fumed behind him. Jan Steen knew well that with a dog, in such circumstances, one must be patient though the skies fall. At last Dirck's grin widened, his tail wagged violently, and his low whining gave way to a bark of elation.

"He's got it," said Jan, with slow satisfaction. He waved his arm, and the two dogs dashed off as if they had been shot out of a gun, keeping close along the inner base of the dyke.

"Dirck's got it," repeated Jan, with conviction, "and nothing will put it out of his head till he's done the job."

II

Side by side, racing wildly like children just let out from school, the two dogs dashed off through the grass along the base of the dyke. Leo, the lighter in build and in colour, and the more conspicuous by reason of a white fore-leg, was also the lighter in spirits. Glad to be clear of the harness and proud of his errand, he was so ebullient in his gaiety that he could spare time to spring into the air now and again and snap at a low-fluttering butterfly. The more phlegmatic Dirck, on the other hand, was too busy keeping his errand fixed in his mind to waste any interest on butterflies, though he was ready enough to gambol a bit whenever his volatile comrade frolicked into collision with him.

Soon--Leo leading, as usual--they quitted the dyke and started off across the open meadows toward the hottest of the firing. A couple of patrolling Uhlans, some distance off to the right, caught sight of them, and a bullet whined complainingly just over their heads. But the other Uhlan, the one who had not fired, rebuked his companion for wasting ammunition. "Can't you see they're just a couple of puppies larking round?" he asked scornfully. "Suppose you thought they were Red Cross."

"Thought they might be dispatch dogs, Herr Sergeant," answered the trooper deprecatingly.

"Well, they're not, blockhead," grunted the cocksure sergeant. And the two rode on, heading diagonally toward the canal.

The dogs, at the sound of the passing bullet, had crouched flat to the ground.

When the sound was not repeated, however, they sprang up and continued their journey, Leo, excited but not terrified, more inclined to frolic than ever, while Dirck, who by some obscure instinct had realized that the shot was not a chance one, but a direct personal attack, kept looking back and growling at the pair of Uhlans.

But though Leo, the exuberant, gambolled as he ran, he ran swiftly, none the less, so swiftly that plodding Dirck had some trouble to keep up with him. Ten minutes more, and they ran into the zone of fire. Bullets hummed waspishly over them, but, after a moment's hesitation, they raced on, flattening themselves belly to earth. The German infantry were in position, quite hidden from view, some six or seven hundred yards to the right. They were firing at an equally invisible line of Belgians, who were occupying a drainage ditch some three hundred yards to the left. The two dogs had no way of knowing that the force on their left was a friendly one, so they kept straight on beneath the crossfire. Had they only known, their errand might have been quickly accomplished.

A little farther on, the grass-land came to an end, and there was a naked, sun-baked stubble-field to cross. As the two raced out over this perilous open space, the battle deepened above them. The fire from the Belgian side went high over the dogs' heads, seeking the far-off target of the enemy's prostrate lines. But the German fire was sighted for too close a range, and the bullets were falling short. Here and there one struck with a vicious spat close to the runners' feet. Here and there a small stone would fly into the air with a sudden inexplicable impulse, or a bunch of stubble would hop up as if startled from its root-hold. A ball just nicked the extreme tip or Dirck's tail, making him think a hornet had stung him. With a surprised yelp, he turned and bit at his supposed assailant. Realizing his mistake in a second, he drooped the injured member sheepishly and tore on after Leo, who had by now got a score of paces ahead.

Next moment a shrapnel shell burst overhead with a shattering roar. Both dogs cowered flat, shivering. There was a smart patter all about them, and little spurts of dust, straw, and dry earth darted upwards. The shrapnel shell was doubtless a mere stray, an ill-calculated shot exploding far from its target. But to Leo it seemed a direct attack upon himself. And well he knew what was the proper thing to do under such circumstances. Partly by instruction, partly by natural sagacity, he had assimilated the vital precept: "When the firing gets too hot, dig yourself in." With his powerful fore-paws he attacked the stubble, making the dry earth fly as if he were trying to dig out a badger. Dirck watched him wonderingly for a moment or two, till a venomous swarm of bullets just over his head seemed to let light in upon his understanding. He fell to copying Leo with vehement enthusiasm. In a brief space each dog had a burrow deep enough to shelter him. Dirck promptly curled himself up in his, and fell to licking his wounded tail. But Leo, burning to get on with his errand, kept bobbing up his head every other second to see how the bullets were striking.

Another shrapnel shell burst in the air, but farther away than the first, and Leo marked where the little spurts of dust arose. They were well behind him. The rifle bullets pinging overhead were higher now, as the Germans were getting the range of the Belgian line. The coast seemed clear enough. He scrambled from his hole and dashed onward down the field, yelping for Dirck to follow. And Dirck was at his heels in half a second.

The tiny canal-side village which was the goal of these two devoted messengers was by this time less than a mile away and straight ahead. When they left it with the machine-gun that morning, it had seemed a little haven of peace. Now the battle was raging all about it. The tall church spire, which had risen serenely above its embosoming trees, had vanished, blown off by a shell. A cottage was burning merrily. Those harmless-looking puffs of cotton-wool were opening out plenteously above the clustered roofs. But all these things made no difference to these two four-footed dispatch-bearers who carried the destiny of the bridge beneath their collars. They had been ordered to take their dispatches to the village, and to the village they would go, whether it had become an inferno or not.

But now the spectacle of the two dogs racing desperately toward the village under the storm of lead and shell had caught the attention of both sides. There was no mistaking them now for frolicsome puppies. There was no question, either, as to which side they belonged to. The German bullets began to lash the ground like hail all about them. Leo, true to his principles, stopped at a tiny depression and once more, with feverish eagerness, began to dig himself in. The earth flew from his desperate paws. In another minute he would have achieved something like cover. But a German sharpshooter got the range of him exactly. A bullet crashed through his sagacious brain, and he dropped, with his muzzle between his legs, into his half-dug burrow.

But Dirck, meanwhile, had for once refused to follow his leader's example. His goal was too near. He saw the familiar uniforms. Above the din he could detect the cries and calls of encouragement from his people. Every faculty in his valiant and faithful being bent itself to the accomplishment of his errand. The bullets raining about him concerned him not at all. The crash of a shrapnel shell just over him did not even make him cock an eye skyward. The shrapnel bullets raised jets of dust before and behind him and on either side. But not one touched him. He knew nothing of them. He only knew his lines were close ahead, and he must reach them.

The Belgians cheered and yelled, and poured in a concentrated fire on that section of the enemy which was attacking the dog. For a few seconds that small, insignificant, desperate four-footed shape drew upon itself the undivided attention of several thousand men. It focussed the battle for the moment. It was only a brindled dog, yet upon its fate hung immense and unknown issues. Every one knew now that the devoted animal was carrying a message. The Germans suddenly came to feel that to prevent the delivery of that message would be like winning a battle. The Belgians turned a battery from harrying a far-off squadron of horse to shell the lines opposite, in defence of the little messenger. Men fell by the score on both sides to decide that unexpected contest.

And still Dirck raced on, heedless of it all.

Then, within fifty yards of the goal, he fell. A bullet had smashed one of his legs. He picked himself up again instantly and hobbled forward, trailing the mangled limb. But the moment he fell, a score of riflemen had leapt from their lines and dashed out to rescue him. Three dropped on the way out. Half a dozen more fell on the way back. But Dirck, whining and licking his rescuers' hands, was carried to shelter behind the massive stone wall of the inn yard, where the Brigadier and his officers were receiving and sending out dispatches.

An aide drew the message from under Dirck's collar and handed it, with a word of explanation, to the General. The latter read it, glanced at the time on the dispatch and then at his watch, and gave hurried orders for strong reinforcements to be rushed up to the old bridge. Then he looked at Dirck, whose shattered leg was being dressed by an orderly.

"That dog," he growled, "has been worth exactly three regiments to us. He's saved the bridge and he's saved three regiments from being cut off. See that he's well looked after, and cured as soon as possible. He's a good soldier, and we'll want him again."

The Calling of the Lop-horned Bull

I

The harvest moon hung globed and honey-coloured over the glassy wilderness lake. In the unclouded radiance the strip of beach and the sand-spit jutting out from it were like slabs of pure ivory between the mirroring steel-blue of the water and the brocaded dark of the richly-foliaged shore.

Behind a screen of this rich foliage--great drooping leaves of water-ash and maple--sat the figure of a man with his back against a tree, almost indistinguishable in the confusion of velvety shadows. His rifle leaning against the tree-trunk beside him, a long, trumpet roll of birch-bark in his hands, he peered forth through the leaves upon the shining stillness, while his ears listened so intently that every now and then they would seem to catch the whisper of his own blood rushing through his veins. But from the moonlit wilds came not a sound except, from time to time, that vast, faint, whispering sigh, inaudible to all but the finest ears, in which the ancient forest seems to breathe forth its content when there is no wind to jar its dreams.

Joe Peddler had settled himself in a comfortable position in his hiding-place in order that he might not have to move. He was out to call moose, and he knew the need of stillness. He knew how far and how inexplicably the news of an intruder would travel through the wild; but he knew also how quickly the wild forgets that news, if only the intruder has craft enough to efface himself. If only he keeps quite still for a time, the vigilant life of the wild seems to conclude that he is dead, and goes once more about its furtive business.

Presently Joe Peddler reached out for his rifle and laid it across his knees.

Then he raised the trumpet of birch-bark to his lips and uttered through it the strange, hoarse cry of the cow-moose calling to her mate. It was a harsh note and discordant, a sort of long-drawn, bleating bellow; yet there was a magic in its uncouth appeal which made it seem the one appropriate voice of those rude but moon-enchanted wilds.

Joe Peddler was such an expert with the birch-bark horn that his performance with it could deceive not only the bull, but also the wary cow, or a cow-stalking bear, or, at times, even an experienced and discriminating fellow-woodsman. He would call twice or thrice, and stop and listen for several minutes, confident that on such a glamorous night as this he would not have long to wait for a response to his lying call.

And he had not. When the bull-moose comes to the call of the cow, he comes sometimes noisily and challengingly, with a crashing of underbrush and a defiant thrashing of his great antlers upon branch and tree as he pounds through them. At other times he comes as softly as the flight of an owl.

Peddler looked out upon the empty whiteness of the beach. He dropped his eyes for a second to the velvet shadows beside him, where a wood-mouse, blundering almost upon his outstretched leg, had fled with a tiny squeak of terror. When he looked out again, there in the centre of the beach, black and huge against the pallid radiance, towered a moose bull, with his great overhanging muzzle uplifted as he peered about him in search of the utterer of that call.

The great bull had a noble pair of antlers, a head for any hunter to be proud of, but Joe Peddler never raised his rifle. Instead of rejoicing at this response to his deceitful lure, a frown of impatience crossed his face. The strict New Brunswick game laws allowed but one bull in a season to fall to the rifle of any one hunter. Joe Peddler was in search of one particular bull. He had no use for the great beast towering so arrogantly before him, and nothing was further from his thoughts than to put a bullet into that wide-antlered head.

The bull was plainly puzzled at finding no cow upon the beach to greet him, after all those calls. Presently he grew angry, perhaps thinking that a rival had reached the scene ahead of him. He fell to pawing the sand with one great, clacking hoof, grunting and snorting so loudly that any rival within half a mile of the spot would have heard him and hastened to accept the challenge. Then he strode up to the nearest bush and began thrashing at it viciously with his antlers.

The disappointed animal now had his back toward the thicket wherein Peddler lay hidden. Yielding to his humour, the woodsman once more lifted the birch-bark tube to his lips, with a sly grin, and gave another call.

He was hardly prepared for the effect. The bull wheeled like a flash, and instantly, with not a half second's hesitation, came charging upon the thicket at full run.

The situation was an awkward one, and Peddler cursed himself for a blundering idiot. He sprang noiselessly to his feet and raised his rifle. But first he would try an experiment, in the hope of saving the beast from his bullet.

"You git out o' that!" he ordered very sharply and clearly. "Git, I tell ye!"

The bull stopped so abruptly that his hooves ploughed up the sand. Decidedly there was something very strange about that thicket. First it gave forth the call of his mate. Then it spoke to him with the voice of a man. And there was something in that voice that chilled him. While one might, perhaps, count ten, he stood there motionless, staring at the inexplicable mass of foliage. The arrogant light in his eyes flickered down into fear. And then, his heart crumbling with panic, he leapt aside suddenly with a mighty spring and went crashing off through the woods as if all the fiends were clawing at his tail.

Peddler chuckled, stretched himself, and settled down to try his luck again. For another couple of hours he kept it up patiently, calling at intervals, and throwing his utmost art into the modulations of the raucous tube. But never a reply could he charm forth from the moonlit solitudes. At last he grew intolerably sleepy.

"Guess old lop-horn must be off on some other beat to-night," he muttered, getting to his feet with a mighty yawn. "It's me fer me bunk." And with the rifle under one arm, the birch-bark tube under the other, he strode off down the shining beach to the alder-fringed inlet where his canoe was hidden.

As he paddled swiftly through the moonlight down toward the lower end of the lake, where he had his camp on a high, dry knoll beside the outlet, Peddler mused upon the object of his quest. It was no ordinary moose, however noble of antler, that had brought him out here to the remote and all but unknown tangle of lakes and swamps which formed the source of the north fork of the Ottanoonsis. This bull, according to the stories of two Indian trappers, was of a size quite unprecedented in the annals of the modern moose; and Peddler, who had seen its mighty hoof-prints in the mud beside the outlet, was quite ready to credit the tale. They were like the tracks of a prehistoric monster. But it was not for the stature of him that Peddler was hunting the giant bull. According to the story of the Indians, the beast's antlers were like those of no other bull-moose ever seen. The right antler was colossal in its reach and spread, a foot or more, at least, beyond the record, but quite normal in its shape. The left, on the contrary, was not only dwarfed to less than half the normal size, but was so fantastically deformed as to grow downwards instead of upwards. Of a head such as this, Joe Peddler was determined to possess himself before some invading sportsman from England or the States should forestall him.

Arriving at the outlet of the lake, he pulled up the canoe at a natural grassy landing-place below his camp, and pushed his way some hundred yards or so along the shore through the bushes to a spring which he had discovered that morning. Your woodsman will go far out of his way to drink at a cold spring, having a distaste for the rather vapid water of the lakes and streams. He threw himself flat upon the stony brink and reached down his thirsty lips.

But just as he swallowed the first delicious gulp of coolness, there came a sudden huge crashing in the brushwood behind him. In one breath he was on his feet. In the next he had cleared the pool in a leap, and was fleeing madly for the nearest tree, with a moose that looked as big as an elephant at his heels.

The nearest tree, a young birch, was not as big as he could have wished, but he was not taking time just then to pick and choose. He whirled himself round the trunk, sprang to the first branch, swung up, and scrambled desperately to gain a safe height. He gained it, but literally by no more than a hair's breadth.

As the black monster reached the tree, it checked itself abruptly, and in almost the same instant lifted its right fore-hoof high above its head and struck like a flash at Peddler's foot just disappearing over a branch. It missed the foot itself, but it shaved the stout cowhide larrigan that covered the foot, slicing it as if with a knife. Peddler drew himself farther up and then looked down upon his assailant with interest.

"I guess I've found ye all right, old lop-horn," he drawled, and spat downward, not scornfully, but contemplatively, as if in recognition, upon that strangely stunted and deformed left antler. "But gee! Them Injuns never said nothin' about yer bein' so black an' so almighty spry. I wisht, now, ye'd kindly let me go back to the canoe an' git me gun!"

But any such quixotic courtesy seemed far from the giant's intention. As soon as he realized that his foe was beyond the reach of striking hoof or thrusting antler, he set himself, in the pride of his strength and weight, to the task of pushing the tree over. Treating it as if it were a mere sapling, he reared himself against it, straddling it with his fore-legs, and thrust at it furiously in the effort to ride it down. As the slim young trunk shook and swayed beneath the passion of the onslaught, Peddler clung to his perch with both arms and devoutly wished that he had had time to choose a sturdier refuge.

For perhaps five minutes the giant pushed and battered furiously against the tree, grunting like a locomotive and tearing up the earth in furrows with his hinder hooves. At length, however, he seemed to conclude that this particular tree was too strong for him. He backed off a few yards and stood glaring up at Peddler among the branches, snorting contemptuously and shaking his grotesquely misshapen antlers as if daring his antagonist to come down. Peddler understood the challenge just as clearly as if it had been expressed in plainest King's English.

"Oh, yes," said he grimly, "I'll come down all right, bime-by. An' ye ain't agoin' to like it one leetle bit when I do; now, mind, I'm tellin' ye!"

For perhaps a half-hour the giant bull continued to rave and grunt and paw about the tree with a tireless vindictiveness which filled his patient prisoner with admiration, and hardened him inexorably in his resolve to possess himself of that unparalleled pair of antlers. At last, however, the furious beast stopped short and stood motionless, listening intently. Peddler wondered what he was listening to. But presently his own ears also caught it--the faint and far-off call of a cow-moose from the upper end of the lake. Forgetting his rage against Peddler, the bull wheeled about with the agility of a cat and went crashing off up the lake shore as fast as he could run. Stiff and chilled--for the air of that crisp October night had a searching bite in it--Peddler climbed down from his perch. First, being tenacious of purpose, he hurried to the spring and finished his interrupted drink. Then, returning to the canoe, he stood for a few moments in hesitation. Should he follow up the trail at once? But it was already near morning, and he was both dead-tired and famished. He believed that the bull, not being in any alarm, would not journey far that night after meeting his mate, but rather would seek some deep thicket for a few hours' sleep. He picked up the rifle and strode off to his camp, resolved to fortify himself well for a long trail on the morrow.

II

Wise though Peddler was in the ways of the wild folk, he found himself at fault in regard to this particular bull, whose habits seemed to be no less unique than his stature and his antlers. Taking up the trail soon after sunrise, he came in due time to the spot, near the head of the lake, where the bull had joined the calling cow. From this point the trail of the pair had struck straight back from the lake towards the range of low hills which formed the watershed between the eastern and south-westward flowing streams. About noon Peddler came to the place where the cow, wearied out by so strenuous a pace, had lain down to sleep in a thicket. The bull, however, driven by his vehement spirit, had gone on without a pause.

All day Peddler followed doggedly upon that unwavering trail. He crossed the ridge, descended to the broken and desolate eastern levels, and came, towards sunset, upon another wide and tranquil lake. Feeling sure that his quarry, unaware of the pursuit, would linger somewhere about this pleasant neighbourhood, Peddler found himself a mossy nest on the cup-shaped top of a boulder and settled down for a couple of hours' sleep. He little guessed that the bull, having doubled back on a parallel with his own trail, had been following him stealthily for a good half hour, not raging now, but consumed with curiosity.

Just as the moon was rising over the low black skyline, jagged with fir-tops, Peddler woke up. Creeping through the bushes, he betook himself to a hiding-place which his quick eye had already marked down, close to the beach, a roomy, flat ledge at the foot of a rock, with a screen of young spruce before it. From behind another clump of spruce, not fifty paces distant, the lop-horned bull, standing moveless as a dead tree, watched him with an intense and inquiring interest. His fury of the preceding night, and even the memory of it, seemed to have been blotted from his mind.

But when, a few minutes later, from that shadowy covert, where he could just make out the crouching form of the man, the call of a cow breathed forth upon the stillness, the great bull's eyes and nostrils opened wide in amazement. What could a moose-cow be thinking about to remain so near the dangerous neighbourhood of a man? But, no, his eyes assured him that there was no cow in the man's hiding-place. Where, then, could she be? He stared around anxiously. She was nowhere in sight. He sniffed the windless night air. It bore no savour of her. He waved forward his great, sensitive ears to listen. And again came the call, the voice, undoubtedly, of the moose-cow.

There could be no question about it this time. It came from the thicket. Had there been any least note of fear in that call, the giant bull would have rushed at once to the rescue of the unseen fair, concluding that the man had her hidden. But now, the utterance was simply that of an untroubled cow. Therefore, for the moment, the great bull was chiefly puzzled. Keeping within the shadows, and moving as imperceptibly as if he were himself but one of the blackest of them, he stole nearer and nearer yet, till he could plainly see every detail within the man's hiding-place. There was assuredly nothing there but rock and moss and bush and the crouching figure of the man himself, staring forth upon the moonlit beach and holding a curious roll of bark to his mouth. Nevertheless, in that same moment there came again the hoarse cry of the cow.

It came indisputably from that crouching form of a man, from that roll of bark at the man's mouth.

This was a mystery, and the wiry black hair along the neck and shoulders of the bull began to rise ominously. A slow, wondering rage awoke in his heart.

It was that element of wonder alone which for the moment restrained him from rushing forward and trampling the mysterious cheat beneath his hooves. A red spark kindled in his eyes.

All undreaming of the dread watcher so close behind him, Peddler set his lips to the lying tube of bark and gave his call again and yet again, with all the persuasiveness of his backwoods art. He felt sure that his efforts were convincing. They were, indeed, all of that. They were so consummate a rendering of the cow-moose's voice that they perfectly convinced a huge and hungry bear, which was at that moment creeping up from the other side of the rock upon the unsuspecting hunter's hiding-place.

The bear knew that its only chance of capturing so swift and nimble a quarry as the moose-cow lay in stealing upon her like a cat and taking her by surprise in one instantaneous rush. He never doubted for a moment that the cow was there behind the rock. When he was within a dozen feet of those persuasive sounds, his crouched form suddenly rose up, elongated itself like a dark and terrible jack-in-the-box, and launched itself with a swish through the encircling branches.

Before Peddler's wits had time fully to take in what was happening, his trained instinct told him what to do. Half rising to his feet as he snatched up his rifle, he swung about and fired from the hip at the vague but monstrous shape which hung for an instant above him. The shot went wide, for just as his finger pressed the trigger, a great black paw smote the weapon from his grasp and hurled it off among the bushes.

With a contortion that nearly dislocated his neck, Peddler hurled himself frantically backwards and aside, and so just escaped the pile-driver descent of the other paw.

He escaped it for the instant; but in the effort he fell headlong, and jammed himself in a crevice of the rock so awkwardly that he could not at once extricate himself. He drew up his legs with an involuntary shudder, and held his breath, expecting to feel the merciless claws rake the flesh from his thighs.

But nothing touched him; and the next moment there broke out an astounding uproar behind him, a very pandemonium of roars and windy gruntings, while the crashing of the bushes was as if the forest were being subdued beneath a steam-roller. Consumed with amazement, he wrenched himself from the crevice and glanced round. The sight that met his eyes made him clamber hastily to the top of the rock, whence he might look down from a more or less safe distance upon a duel of giants such as he had never dared hope to witness.

When the bear found that it was no cow-moose, but a man that he was springing upon, he was so taken aback that, for a second or two, he forbore to follow up his advantage. To those two seconds of hesitation Joe Peddler owed his escape.

Before the massive brute, now boiling with rage at having been so deceived, had sufficiently made up his mind to fall upon that prostrate figure in the crevice, something that seemed to him like a tornado of hooves and antlers burst out of the bushes and fell upon him. The next moment, with a long, red gash half-way down his flank, he was fighting for his life.

The gigantic moose had been just upon the verge of rushing in to silence those incomprehensible and deceiving calls, when the towering form of the bear burst upon his vision. Here at last was something to focus his wrath. Already angry, but still dampened by bewilderment, his anger now exploded into a very madness of rage. There was the ancient, inherited feud between his tribe and all bears. As a youngster, he had more than once escaped, as by a miracle, from the neck-breaking paw of a bear, had more than once seen a young cow struck down and ripped to pieces. Now to this deep-seated hate was added another incentive. His mind confused by fury to protect his mate, he dimly felt that the mystery which had been tormenting him was the fault of this particular bear. The man was forgotten. A cow had been calling to him. She had disappeared. Here was the bear. The bear had probably done away with the cow. The cow should be terribly avenged.

The bear--which was one of the biggest and fiercest of his kind in all the northern counties--had fought moose, both bulls and cows, before. But he had never before faced such an antagonist as this one, and that first slashing blow from the bull's knife-edged fore-hoof had somewhat flurried him. Sitting back poised, with his immense hindquarters gathered under him, and his fore-paws uplifted, he parried the smashing strokes of his assailant with the lightning dexterity of a trained boxer. His strength of shoulder and forearm was so enormous that if he could have got a stroke in flat, at right angles to the bone, he would have shattered the bull's leg to splinters. But his parrying blows struck glancingly, and did no more than rip the hair and hide.

After a few minutes of whirlwind effort to batter down that impregnable guard, the bull jumped back as nimbly, for all his bulk, as a young doe startled from her drinking. His usual method of attack, except when fighting a rival bull, was to depend upon his battering fore-hooves. But now he changed his tactics. Lowering his head so that his vast right antler stood out before him like a charge of bayonets, he launched himself full upon his adversary.

With all his weight and strength behind it, that charge was practically irresistible, if fairly faced. But the bear was too wise to face it fairly. He swung aside, clutched the lowered antler, and held fast, striving to pull his enemy down.

But the bull's strength and impetus were too great, and the bear was himself thrown off his balance. Even then, however, he might probably have recovered himself and once more established the battle upon even terms. But he had not reckoned--he could not have been expected to reckon--upon the unprecedented weapon of that little down-drooping left antler. Not for nothing was the giant bull lop-horned. The dwarfed and distorted antler hung down like a plough-share. And the bear attempted no defence against it. Keen-spiked, it caught him in the belly and ploughed upward. In a paroxysm he fell backwards. The bull, swinging his hindquarters around without yielding his advantage for a second, lunged forward with all his force, and the deadly little plough was driven home to the bear's heart.

Peddler, from his post on top of the rock, shouted and applauded in wild excitement, and showered encomiums, no less profane than heartfelt, upon the victorious bull. For a minute or two the bull paid no attention, being engrossed in goring and trampling his victim in an effort to make it look less like a bear than an ensanguined floor-rug. At last, as if quite satisfied with his triumph, he lifted his gory head and eyed that voluble figure on top of the rock. It looked harmless.

"Gee, but ye kin fight!" said Peddler, glowing with admiration. "An' ye've saved my scalp fer me this night, fer sartain. Guess I'll hev to let ye keep them lop-sided horns o' yourn, after all!"

The bull snorted at him scornfully and turned his head to take another prod at the unresponsive remnants of his foe. Then, paying no further heed to the man on the rock, and craving assuagement to the fiery smart of his wounds, he strode down into the lake and swam straight out, in the glitter of the moon-path, toward the black line of the farther shore.

The Aigrette

The Girl, sitting before her dressing-table, looked at the fair reflection in her great mirror and smiled happily. Those searching lights at either side of the mirror could find no flaw in the tender colouring of her face, in the luminous whiteness of neck and arm and bosom. Her wide-set eyes, like the red bow of her mouth, were kind and gay. The brightness of her high-coiffed hair was surmounted by a tuft of straight egret plumes, as firm, pearl-white, and delicate as a filigree of frost.

The Girl had never looked so lovely. Never before had she worn anything that so became her as that ethereal plume. She knew it; and the glances of her maid, straying from her business with filmy garments and dainty adornments, told her so. She threw a wisp of silken gossamer over her arm and tripped eagerly down to the drawing-room.

The Man came forward to meet her, his eyes paying without stint the tribute she was craving of him.

"There will be no one there to compare with you!" he said softly. "There is no one anywhere to compare with you."

"It is becoming, isn't it?" she answered, glowing at his praise, and nodding her bright head to indicate the ethereal white plume.

"It is indeed," he asserted heartily. "But nothing could heighten your beauty. You did not need it, and I'm rather afraid the bird did." He kissed her finger-tips as he spoke, lest she should think he was being critical.

The Girl pouted a little, being very tenderhearted, and loth to be reminded of unpleasant things.

"I know what you mean," said she quickly, withdrawing her hand in displeasure. "But the poor bird is dead, anyway; and if I didn't buy the thing, some other woman would. And it's horrid of you to speak of it now!"

The Man laughed.

"It can't make you more beautiful, but if it makes you happier, that's quite enough for me," said he. "I'm afraid that a very little pleasure for you is of more consequence in my eyes than a thousand million birds."

And upon this assurance the Girl forgave him.

* * * * *

The wide lagoon lay windless, shining like milky-blue glass under the blaze of the southern sky. It was shallow, its surface broken here and there with patches of tall gold-green reeds. Its shores seemed half afloat, fringed as they were with gnarled, squat bushes growing directly out of the water. This irregular bushy growth, with the green-shadowed water beneath its branches, stretched back for several hundred yards from the open lagoon to a dense wall of jungle, a banked mass of violently green leafage starred with cream-white and crimson bloom.

Not cream-white, but of a coldly pure silver-white, like new snow, some two or three score long-necked, long-legged birds flapped angularly between the milky blue of the water and the intense, vibrant blue of the sky, or stood half-leg deep in the shallows, motionless, watching for their prey. They looked like bits of a Japanese screen brought to life and sown broadcast in this sun-steeped southern wilderness. High overhead, a black speck against the azure, a hawk wheeled slowly in vast spirals, staring down desirously upon the peaceful lagoon. That peace he durst not invade, for he knew and feared the lightning strokes of the long dagger-like beaks of the white egrets.

In the top of one of the gnarled bushes at the edge of the open, right over the water, was built a spacious but rickety-looking nest of dead sticks. It was the most un-nestlike of nests, a mere crazy platform, with no apparent qualifications as a home except the most perfect ventilation. One might reasonably suppose that the first requirement in the nest of a bird should be that it would hold eggs securely. But this unsightly collection of sticks looked as if that was the last thing it could be depended on to do. It was so loose and open that the eggs ought to fall through into the water. It was so flat that any eggs which dodged falling through should surely, according to all known laws of Nature, be blown off by the first vigorous gust. Nevertheless, it was clear that the rude structure had held eggs, and proved not unworthy of its trust, for it was now occupied by four young egrets.

They were grotesque and solemn babies, these nestlings, sitting up quite motionless on their leg-joints and half-feathered rumps, with their long legs thrust straight out before them over the sticks, their long beaks resting contemplatively on their nearly naked breasts, their round, bright, unwinking eyes staring out blankly upon their little world of gold and blue. Scattered here and there over the sweep of fringing bushes were a dozen or so more of these rickety platforms of sticks, each with its solemn group of stilt-legged staring young, motionless as statues interested in nothing upon earth save the quantity of fish or frogs which their untiring parents could supply to their unassuageable appetites.

Above this outermost nest, with the four fledglings in it, hung for a moment, hovering on wide wings, the great white mother egret, with a shining orange fish in her beak. She dropped her long legs, as if feeling for a foothold, and alighted on the edge of the crazy platform so softly that not a stick protested. At her coming four long beaks were lifted into the air, gaping hungrily and squawking with eagerness. All four seemed equally ravenous. But the mother-bird knew well enough which she had fed last, and which was most in need. She jammed the prize, with what seemed scant ceremony, into the beak whose turn it was to get it. The fish was thicker than the youngster's long thin neck, but it was promptly swallowed head first. It went down slowly, with a succession of spasms which looked agonizing, but were, in fact, ecstatic.

Before flying off again to resume her quest of fish, the mother egret remained for a few moments on the edge of the nest, to rest and preen herself. Her snow-pure plumage shone in the sunlight like spun silver. Her neck feathers were prolonged in fine drooping lines far down over her breast. From the centre of her back, between the shoulders, grew a bunch of long, exquisitely delicate plumes, as white and apparently as fragile as the frost-flowers on a window. These were her festal adornment, worn, by herself and her mate alike, only in the nesting season.

Having preened herself well, and shaken her long, snaky neck as if to take the kinks out of it, she spread her shining wings and lifted herself into the air. She rose, however, but a few inches, and then, flapping and squawking wildly, she was dragged down again by some unseen force. Her frantic struggles knocked off a corner of the nest, and swept off one of the awkward nestlings, which fell kicking and sprawling through the leafage and disappeared with a splash. A moment more and the mother, for all her wild fight against the unseen fate, was drawn down after him into the shadowed water. Then a little flat-bottomed boat, or ducking-punt, with a man crouching in the bottom of it, came worming its way through the narrow lane of water between the stems of the bushes. The man seized her by the dangerous beak, jerked her into the punt, put his knee upon her neck, detached the noose of a copper-wire snare from her leg, drew a keen hunting-knife, and deftly sliced the snowy plumes from the flesh of her back.

Then he hurled her out into the open water, that she might not be in his way while he rearranged the snare upon the edge of the nest in order to catch her mate.

Half stunned, and altogether bewildered by her agony, the mother egret flapped blindly upon the top of the water, her snowy plumage crimsoned with her life-blood. After a few moments she succeeded in getting into the air. Flying heavily, and lurching as she went, she flew across the lagoon, blundered in among the bushes, and fell with her legs in the water, her twitching wings entangled in the branches. There, after a few vain struggles, she lay still, dying slowly--very slowly--her beak half open, but her eyes wide and undaunted.

Not long afterwards the male egret, who had been fishing far down the lagoon, and knew nothing of what had happened, came back to the nest with food. He, too, was caught in the fatal snare, dragged down, scalped of his nuptial plumes as the red savage of old scalped his enemies, and thrown away to die at his leisure. The law of that country forbade the shooting of the egrets in the nesting season, when alone they wore the plumes which women crave. The plume-hunter, therefore, felt that he was evading the law successfully if he hacked the prize from the living bird and released it while still alive and able to fly. If the bird died agonizingly afterwards, who was going to swear that he was the slayer?

Throughout the morning the like swift tragedy was enacted at one nest after the other. The deadly punt slid murderously, silently, up and down the hidden water-lanes among the bushes, and the man with the knife did his work noiselessly, save for the threshing and splashing of his victims.

In the course of an hour, however, for all the marauder's stealth, the whole herony was in a state of desperate fear. Half a dozen birds had been snared, and the others, flying high overhead and staring down with keen, terrified eyes, had detected the slaughterer in his hiding under the branches. They had seen him, too, resetting his snares upon the edges of the nests. And in spite of the fact that, after doing so, he withdrew to some distance among the bushes--as far as the cords attached to the snares would permit--they dreaded to approach their nests again. But there were their younglings, solemn and hungry, quite uncomprehending of the doom which hung over them, hoarsely and trustingly petitioning to be fed. The parent birds could not long resist those appeals. Love and tenderness triumphed over fear, even over the clear view of mortal peril. One after another the great white birds came back, trembling but devoted, to their nests. One after another, sooner or later, got a foot into that implacable wire noose, was dragged down beneath the bushes, and thrown out weltering in its blood. There was no escaping a trap thus baited with the appeals of the young. And before the lagoon had taken the first of the sunset colour, there was not one adult egret in the whole herony which had not paid the bloody price of its devotion.

At last, when the lagoon lay like a sheet of burnished copper, the man with the punt came out boldly from among the bushes and paddled off toward the outlet with his bleeding trophies. As he vanished, three or four birds, stronger and more tenacious of life than their fellows, came flapping back to their nests, their backs and wings and thighs caked with blood. Swaying as they perched upon the stick platforms, they managed to feed the nestlings once more. Then, dogged in their devotion, they flew off to continue their tasks.

They never returned again, but fell in the shallows where they stood trying to fish: and if the Fates of the wilderness elected to be merciful, they were drowned quickly.

All night, through the star-strewn summer dark, the orphaned nestlings kept up their harshly plaintive cries of hunger and loneliness. A pair of owls, hearing these cries, and guessing that all could not be right with the egret colony, came winnowing up noiselessly and took toll of the defenceless nests. After daybreak, the wheeling hawk dropped low to investigate, then struck wherever he found the nestlings fattest and most tempting. Toward noon, under the pitiless downpour of the unclouded sun, the little ones wilted like cut grass, thirst and hunger stilling their pitiful complaints. Long before night there was not a nestling left alive on the whole lagoon.

* * * * *

The Girl, with snowy aigrette in her bright hair, her gloved fingers resting on the Man's arm, stood upon the kerb outside the theatre, waiting for a taxi. A light dogcart came by. The horse, sleek and spirited and spoilt, was in wayward humour, and took it into its head to give its driver trouble. The driver tried to soothe it, but it would not be soothed. It began backing capriciously. The driver cut it smartly with his light whip.

"Oh," cried the Girl, "see how he's beating that poor horse! What a brute!"

"It's hurting the horse about as much," said the Man, "as if you struck it with your fan! Moreover, the horse is behaving very badly, and must be made to mind. It's endangering the whole traffic."

The Girl flushed, bit her lip, and withdrew her hand from the Man's arm. Just then the summoned taxi drew up at the kerb. The Girl stepped in.

"What brutes men are!" she said. "Perhaps they can't help being cruel! They have no intuition, so how can they understand?"

The Man glanced at the aigrette, smiled discreetly, and said nothing.

The Cabin in the Flood

Stepping into the cabin, Long Jackson said: "If that there blame jam don't break inside o' twenty-four hour, the hull valley's goin' to be under water, an' I'll hev to be gittin' ye out o' this in the canoe. I've just been uncoverin' her an' rozenin' her up, an' she's as good as noo. That's a fine piece o' winter bark ye put on to her, Tom."

From his bunk in the dark corner beyond the stove, Brannigan lifted his shaggy face and peered wistfully out into the sunshine with sunken but shining eyes.

"I was afeard there'd be a powerful freshet after this long spell o' thaw atop of all that rain, Long, an' the snow layin' so deep in the woods this winter. I wisht ye'd lug me over an' lay me by the door in the sun fer a bit, Long, ef 'tain't too much trouble. That 'ere sun'll put new life into me bones, in case the jam don't break, an' we hev to git a move on."

After this long speech, Brannigan's head dropped wearily back on the roll of blanket that served him as pillow. He had been desperately ill with pneumonia, so ill that it had been impossible for Long Jackson to go in to the Settlements for a doctor; and now, under Jackson's assiduous nursing, he was just beginning the slow climb back to life.

"Think 'twon't be too cold fer ye by the door?" queried Jackson anxiously.

"No, no!" protested Brannigan. "It's the sun I'm wantin', and the smell o' spring stirrin' in the buds. That's the med'cine fer me now, Long."

Long Jackson grumbled doubtfully, holding to the strange back-country superstition that fresh air is dangerous for sick folk. But he yielded, as he usually did where Brannigan was concerned. He spread blankets on the floor by the door--a little to one side to avoid the draught--then carried his partner's gaunt form over to them, and rolled him up like a baby, with his head well propped on a pile of skins. Then he seated himself on the chopping-log just outside the door, and proceeded to fill his pipe with that moist, black plug tobacco, good alike for smoking and for chewing, which is chiefly favoured by the backwoodsman. Brannigan's face, drinking in the sunshine as a parched lawn drinks rain, freshened and picked up a tinge of colour. His eyes, long weary of the four grey walls of the cabin, roved eagerly the woods that fringed the tiny clearing.

"Anyways," said Long Jackson between puffs, as he sucked the damp tobacco alight, "this here knoll of ourn's the highest bit o' country fer ten miles round, and the cabin's on the highest p'int of it. 'Tain't raly likely the water'll come clean over it, ef the jam don't give inside o' twenty-four hour. But it makes one feel kind o' safe havin' the canoe ready."

"Yes, it's the highest bit o' country fer miles round," murmured Brannigan dreamily, soaking in the sun. "An' I'm thinkin' we ain't the only ones as knows it, Long. Will ye look at them rabbits down yander? Did ever ye see so many o' them together afore?"

Jackson looked, and involuntarily laid his pipe down on the log beside him to look again. The woods far down the slope--it was a slope so gentle as to be hardly perceptible--were swarming with rabbits, hopping and darting this way and that over the snow. For the snow still lingered under the trees, though only a few patches of it, yellowing and shrinking under the ardent sun, remained in the open of the clearing.

After staring for some moments in silence, Jackson took up his pipe again.

"The water must be risin' mighty quick," said he. "Them rabbits are gittin' sociable all of a sudden. They're comin' to pay ye a call, Tom, this bein' yer fust day up."

"We'll be havin' other callers besides rabbits, I'm thinkin'," said Brannigan, the dreaminess in his voice and eyes giving way to a pleased excitement. This was better than his bunk in the dark corner of the cabin. "What's that, now, way down behind them yaller birch trunks?" he added eagerly. "I guess it's a bear, Long."

"It's two bear," corrected Jackson. "So long as it's jest rabbits, all right, but we ain't entertainin' bears this mornin'. Grub's too scarce, an' bears is hungry this time o' year. Gee! There's two more down by the spring. Guess I'd better git the gun."

"Wait a bit, Long," expostulated Brannigan. "They're so afeard o' the water, they'll be harmless as the rabbits. No good shootin' 'em now, when their pelts ain't worth the skinnin'. Let 'em be, an' see what they'll do. They hain't got no place else to go to, to git out o' the water."

"Let 'em climb a tree!" grumbled Jackson. But he sat down again on his log. "Ye're right, anyhow, Tom," he continued, after a moment's consideration. "What's the good o' spilin' good skins by shootin' 'em now? An' if they're not too skeered to death to know they're hungry, they kin eat the rabbits. An', anyhow, the ca'tridges is pretty nigh gone. Come along, Mr. Bear, an' bring yer wife an' all yer relations!"

As if in response to this invitation, the bears all moved a little nearer, whining uneasily and glancing back over their shoulders, and close behind them could now be seen gleams of the swiftly up-creeping flood, where the sunlight struck down upon it through the leafless hardwood trees. But around to the left and the rear of the cabin the trees were dense evergreens, spruce and fir, beneath whose shade the flood came on unseen.

As the worried bears approached, the belt of rabbits swarmed out along the edges of the clearing, the hinder ranks pushing forward the reluctant front ones. These, fearing the open and the human form sitting before the cabin, tried to regain shelter by leaping back over the heads of those who thrust them on. But far more than that unmoving human figure they feared the whimpering bears and the silent, pursuing flood. So in a very few minutes the rabbits were all in the open, hopping about anxiously and waving their long ears, a few of the bolder ones even coming up to within forty or fifty feet of the cabin to stare curiously at Long Jackson on his log.

Presently from behind the cabin, stepping daintily, with heads held high and wide nostrils sniffing the air apprehensively, came two young does, and stopped short, glancing back and forth from Jackson to the bears, from the bears to Jackson. After a few seconds' hesitation, they seemed to make up their minds that they liked Jackson better than the bears, for they came a few steps nearer and looked timidly in at Brannigan.

"This ain't North Fork Valley, Long. It's Barnum's Menagerie, that's what it's gittin' to be!" remarked Brannigan, speaking softly, lest he should alarm the does.

"Ay, an' still they come!" said Jackson, pointing with his pipe down the slope to the right. Brannigan lifted his head and craned his neck to see who "they" were.

They were a huge bull-moose, followed by three cows and a couple of yearlings, who crowded close upon their leader's heels as they caught sight of the bears. The great bull, though without antlers at this season, haughtily ignored the bears, who, as he well knew, would have small inclination to venture within reach of his battering hoofs. The little herd had been swimming. With dripping flanks, they stalked up through the trees and out into the clearing, the swarm of rabbits parting before them like a wave. At sight of Jackson on his log, the bull stopped and stood staring morosely. He was not afraid of bears, but men were another matter. After a heavy pondering of the situation, he led the way across the corner of the clearing, then down into the flood again and off, heading for the uplands at the foot of the valley, some five or six miles away.

"He don't seem to like the looks o' ye, Long," murmured Brannigan.

"No more'n I do his'n," answered Jackson. "But I guess he'd 'a' been welcome to stop, seein' as we ain't standin' on ceremony, an' our cards is out to everybody. Come one, come all! But, no, I bar Mr. and Mrs. Skunk. Ye're a soft-hearted old eejut, Tom, an' never like to hurt nobody's feelin's, but I do hope now ye didn't go an' send cards to Mr. and Mrs. Skunk."

Brannigan chuckled. He was feeling better and more like himself already.

"I don't believe they'll be comin'," he answered, evading the point of the invitation. "Like as not, they're cut off in their holes an' drownded, 'less they've took to the trees in time. They ain't no great travellers, ye know, Long."

"I ain't puttin' on no mournin' fer 'em," grunted Jackson. "An' there's another varmint ye hadn't no call to invite, Tom," he added, as the rabbits again scattered in consternation, and a big lynx emerged from a spruce thicket on which the flood was just beginning to encroach. The lynx, too frightened at the rising water to give even one look at the rabbits, glared about her with round, pale, savage eyes. As she caught sight of Jackson, her fur fluffed up and she scrambled into the nearest tree, where she crouched behind a branch.

Brannigan spared but a glance for the terrified lynx, his interest being largely absorbed in the two does, whose trustfulness had won his heart. Just inside the cabin door, and within reach of his arm, was a shelf, whereon stood a tin plate containing some cold buckwheat pancakes, or flap-jacks, left over from breakfast. A couple of these he tossed to the does. Gentle as was the action, the nervous beasts bounded backwards, snorting with apprehension. In a few moments, however, as if coming to realize that the movement of Brannigan's arm had not been a hostile one, they came forward again hesitatingly, and at length began to sniff at the pancakes. For some moments the sniffing was distinctly supercilious. Then one of them ventured to nibble. Half a minute more, and both flap-jacks had been greedily gobbled. Their immense, mild eyes plainly asking for more of the novel provender, the pair stepped a little closer. Brannigan reached for another cake, to divide between them.

Long Jackson got up from his log, tapped the ashes from his pipe, and came into the cabin.

"I'll be leavin' ye to entertain the ladies, Tom," said he, "while I git dinner."

II

A cloud passing over the sun, the air grew sharply cold on the instant. Long Jackson bundled Brannigan away from the door, and shut it inexorably. But as Brannigan refused to be put back into his bunk, Jackson arranged him an awkward sort of couch of benches and boxes by the table, where he made his first "sitting-up" meal. After dinner, the sun having come out again, he insisted upon the door being once more thrown open, that he might drink in the medicine of the spring air and have another look at his menagerie.

"Holy Je-hoshaphat!" exclaimed Jackson, as the door swung back. "This ain't no menagerie we've got here, Tom. It's a Noah's Ark, that's what it be!"

The two does, trembling with fright, were huddled against the wall of the cabin, close beside the door, staring at an immense and gaunt-framed bear, which was sitting up on its haunches on Jackson's chopping-block. More than half the clearing was under water. Five more bears sat near the chopping-block, eyeing the water fearfully and whimpering like puppies. Quite near them, and letting his shrewd eyes survey the whole scene with an air of lofty indifference, sat a red fox, his fur bedraggled as if from a long and hard swim. In two compact masses, on either side of the bears and the fox, and as far away from them as they could get, huddled the rabbits, their eyes fairly popping from their heads. Further away, standing hock-deep in the water, were half a dozen more red deer, afraid to come any closer to the bears. In the branches of the one tree--a spreading rock-maple--which had been left standing near the cabin, crouched a lynx and a wild-cat, as far apart as possible, and eyeing each other jealously.

One of the bears, restless in his anxiety, shifted his position and came a little nearer to the cabin. The two does, snorting at his approach, backed abruptly into the doorway, jamming Jackson against the doorpost.

"Oh, don't mind me, ladies!" said Jackson, with elaborate sarcasm. "Come right along in an' set down!"

Whereupon the frightened animals, flying in the face of that tradition of the wild creatures which teaches them to dread anything like a cul-de-sac, took him at his word. Stamping their delicate hoofs in a sort of timorous defiance to the bears, and ignoring both Jackson and Brannigan completely, they backed into the rear of the cabin, stared about the place curiously, and at length fell to nibbling the hay which formed the bedding of the bunks.

"Did ever ye see the likes o' that for nerve?" demanded Jackson.

"They've got sense, them two," said Brannigan. "They know who'll stand up fer 'em if them bears begin to git ugly."

"But we don't want the whole kit an' calabash pilin' in on us," said Jackson with decision. "An' we don't want to shet the door and not be able to see what's goin' on, neether. Guess I'd better fix up a kind o' barricade, so's I kin hold the pass in case of them there fee-rocious rabbits undertakin' to rush us."

With a bench and some boxes, he built a waist-high barrier across the doorway, and then he arranged for Brannigan a couch on the table, so that the invalid could look out comfortably over the barrier.

"Reserved seat in Noah's Ark for ye, Tom," said he.

"Hadn't ye better be fetchin' the canoe round to the front, where ye kin keep an eye onto it?" suggested Brannigan.

"By Jing, yes!" agreed Jackson. "If one of them slick old bears 'd take a notion to h'ist it into the water an' make off in it, I guess we'd be in the porridge."

He hitched his long legs over the barrier and stalked out coolly among the beasts.

The wild-cat and the lynx in the branches overhead laid back their ears and showed their teeth in vicious snarls; and the rabbits huddled so close together that the two packs of them heaved convulsively as each strove to get behind or underneath his neighbours. The bears sullenly drew away to the water's edge, and the huge fellow perched on the chopping-block jumped down nimbly from his perch and joined the others with a protesting woof. The fox stood his ground and kept up his air of indifference, his native shrewdness telling him that the man was paying no heed to him whatever. The deer also did not seem greatly disturbed by Jackson's appearance, merely waving their big ears and staring interrogatively. Jackson picked up the canoe and turned it bottom side up across the doorway. Then he stepped indoors again.

About the middle of the afternoon it became evident that the water had stopped rising. It had apparently found an overflow somehow, and there was no longer any risk of the cabin being swept away. Tired with the excitement, Brannigan fell asleep. And Jackson, with the backwoodsman's infinite capacity for doing nothing, when there is nothing to do, sat beside his barricade for hour after hour and smoked. And for hour after hour nothing happened. When night fell, he shut the door and secured it with special care.

Throughout the night it rained heavily, under a lashing wind which drove the rain in sheets against the rear of the cabin; but soon after dawn the sun came out again and shone with eager warmth. Brannigan awoke so much better that he was able to sit up and help himself to the doorway instead of being carried. The two does, thoroughly at home in the cabin, swallowed the cold pancakes, and kept close to Jackson's elbow, begging for more.

When the door was opened, it was seen that the animals had all been driven round to the front of the cabin for shelter. The space under the upturned canoe was packed with rabbits. But the spirit of the bigger animals, with the exception of the deer, was now changed.

Since the rise of the flood had come to a halt--for the water was at the same mark as on the afternoon of the previous day--the predatory animals had begun to forget their fear of it and to remember that they were hungry. The truce of terror was wearing very thin. The fox, indeed, as Jackson's alert eyes presently perceived, had already broken it. At the very edge of the water, as far away as possible from the cabin and the bears, he was sitting up demurely on his haunches and licking his chaps. But a tell-tale heap of bones and blood-stained fur gave him away. In the darkness he had stolen up to the rabbits, nipped one noiselessly by the neck, and carried it off without any of its fellows being any the wiser. He could afford to wait with equanimity for the flood to go down.

The lynx had come down out of her tree and was crouching at the foot of it, eyeing first the bears and then the rabbits. She turned her tameless, moon-pale eyes upon Jackson in the doorway, and bared her teeth in a soundless snarl. Jackson, wondering what she was up to, kept perfectly still. The next moment she darted forward, belly to earth, and pounced upon the nearest rabbit. The victim screamed amazingly loud, and the packed mass of its companions seemed to boil as they trampled each other underfoot. Growling harshly, the lynx sprang back to the tree with her prey, ran up the trunk with it, and crouched in a crotch to make her meal, keeping a malignant and jealous eye upon the wild-cat on her neighbouring branch.

As if fired by this example, one of the bears made a rush upon the luckless rabbits. He struck down two with a deft stroke of his paw, dashed them to one side to remove them from the too close proximity of Jackson, and lay down comfortably to devour them.

At this second attack, the unfortunate rabbits seemed to wake up to the necessity of doing something radical. Two or three of those nearest the cabin made a sudden dart for the door. They jumped upon the upturned canoe, stared fearfully for an instant at Jackson, then leapt past him over the barrier and took refuge in the farthest corner of the cabin, under the bunk. Jackson, according to his prearranged plan, had made an effort to stop them, but it was a half-hearted effort, and he shook his head at Brannigan with a deprecating grin.

"'Tain't exackly healthy for the blame little scuts, out there with the bear an' the wild-cats," said he apologetically. Jackson was quite ready to shoot rabbits, of course, when they were needed for stew; but his soft, inconsistent heart had been moved at seeing the helpless things mangled by the lynx and the bear. Perfect consistency, after all, would be an unpleasant thing to live with in this excellent but paradoxical world.

The words were hardly out of Jackson's mouth when the rest of the bears came stalking up, great, black, menacing forms, to levy toll upon the rabbits. Instantly the frantic little animals began pouring in a tumultuous stream over the canoe and the barrier and into the cabin. Seeing their dinners thus unexpectedly disappearing, the bears made a rush forward.

Jackson, fearing lest they should charge straight into the cabin, sprang for his gun, and was back in the doorway again in a flash, carelessly thrusting aside with his feet the incoming flood of furry, hopping figures, but making no effort to keep it out.

The bears, reaching the packed and struggling rear rank of the fugitives before it could dissolve and gain the refuge, captured each a victim, and drew back again hastily with their prizes, still apprehensive of the silent grey figure of Jackson in the doorway. And in two minutes more all the rabbits were inside the cabin, covering the floor and struggling with each other to keep from being pushed too close to the hot stove. The two does, resenting the invasion, snorted angrily and struck at them with their sharp, agile hoofs, killing several before the rest learned to keep out of the way. One enterprising little animal sprang into the lower bunk, and was straightway followed by the nearest of his fellows, till the bunk was filled to overflowing.

"How'll ye like it, sleepin' along o' that bunch o' bed-fellers, Tom?" inquired Jackson derisively.

"Ye'll sleep with 'em yourself, Long," retorted Brannigan from his place on the table. "I didn't let 'em in. They're your visitors. Me bein' an invalid, I'm goin' to take the top bunk!"

Long Jackson scratched his head.

"What's botherin' me," said he, grown suddenly serious, "is them bears. If they take it into their heads to come in an' board along of us, I'm goin' to hev a job to stop 'em. I've only four ca'tridge left, an' ther's six bear. They've et ther rabbits, an' what's one small rabbit to a rale hungry bear? Here's the biggest an' hungriest comin' now! Scat!" he yelled fiercely. "Scat! You----!" And he added a string of backwoods objurgation that this modest page would never consent to record.

Apparently abashed at this reception, the bear backed away hastily and glanced around at the landscape as if he had had no least thought of intruding.

Brannigan laughed as he had not laughed for weeks.

"That langwidge o' yourn's better'n any gun, Long!" said he.

"Guess it's saved us one ca'tridge, that time!" he acknowledged modestly. "But I'm thinkin' it won't keep 'em off when they get a mite hungrier. Ye kin curse like an Androscoggin lumber jack, but y'ain't goin' to frizzle a single hair on a bear's hide. Now, here they come agin! I'd better shoot one, an' mebbe that'll discourage 'em. Anyhow, they kin eat the one I shoot, and that'll keep 'em from hankerin' so after rabbits."

He raised his gun, but Brannigan stopped him sharply.

"Jest shet the door, ye old eejut!" he cried. "Ye know as well as I do that ef ye git a bear rale mad, an' he thinks he's cornered, there's goin' to be trouble.

Jest shet the door, that's all!"

"To be sure! Why didn't I think o' that afore?" agreed Jackson, kicking the boxes aside and slamming the heavy door without ceremony in the face of the nearest bear, who had already lifted his fore-paws upon the canoe and was peering in wistfully at the rabbits.

With his feet in a foam of rabbits--the creatures seeming to have lost all fear of him--Jackson sat down on a box and lit his pipe, while Brannigan, leaning over from his couch on the table, tried to feed the rabbits with biscuits. The rabbits would have none of it, but the two does, greedy and jealous, came mincing forward at once to appropriate the attention and the tit-bits.

Presently the air grew unbearably hot and close, with the reek of the crowding animals and the heat of the stove. After the fashion of the backwoodsman, the men endured it till they were gasping. Then Jackson went to the little window--which was not made to open--and prised out the sash with the edge of his axe-blade. He filled his lungs with a deep breath, drew back from the window, then sprang forward again and thrust his head out for a better look.

"It's broke!" he shouted. "The water's goin' down hand over fist!"

"It'll save a lot o' trouble," said Brannigan, with a sigh of relief.

By noon the water had disappeared, and the bears, the wild-cat, and the fox had disappeared with it. After waiting another hour, that the hungry beasts might be well out of the way, Jackson opened the door and began to turn the rabbits out. At first they refused obstinately to go, so that he had to seize them by the ears and throw them out. But presently some sign seemed to go round among them to the effect that their enemies were out of the way. Then they all began to make for the door, but quite at their leisure, and soon were hopping off among the trees in every direction. After them at last, went the two does, without so much as once looking back.

"Durned if the place don't look kind o' lonesome without 'em!" murmured Brannigan.

"Umph!" grunted Jackson. "It's easy seein' 'tain't you that's got to do the cleanin' up after 'em. If ever ye go to hev another party like that, Tom, I'm goin' to quit."

The spring wind, mild and spicy from the spruce forests, breathed through the cabin from the open door to the open window, and a chickadee ran over his fine-drawn, bead-like refrain from the branches where the lynx and wild-cat had been crouching.

The Brothers of the Yoke

Side by side, in the position in which they were accustomed to labour at the yoke--Star on the off side, Buck on the nigh--they stood waiting in the twilight beside the pasture bars. From the alder swamp behind the pasture, coolly fragrant under the first of the dew-fall, came the ethereal fluting of a hermit thrush, most tender and most poignant of all bird songs. In the vault of the pale sky--pale violet washes of thin colour over unfathomable deeps of palest green--a wide-swooping night-hawk sounded at intervals its long, twanging note, like a stricken harpstring. The dark spruce woods beyond the barn began to give off their aromatic balsam-scent upon the evening air. A frog croaked from somewhere under the alders where the hermit was at his fluting. One of the oxen at last began to low softly and anxiously. It was long past watering-time. Immediately his mate repeated the complaint, but on a harsher, more insistent key. The watering trough, full to the brim, was there in full view before them, just at the other side of the cabin. It was an unheard-of thing that their master should not come at sundown to lower the bars and let them drink their fill.

They were a splendid pair, these two steers, and splendidly matched. Both dark red, deep and massive in the shoulder, with short, straight horns, and each with a clean white star in the centre of his broad forehead, they were so exactly alike in all external particulars, that the uninitiated eye would have been puzzled to distinguish them. Both stood also with the patient, bowed necks of those who have toiled long under the burden of the yoke. But to one at all acquainted with animals, at all versed in the psychology of the animal mind, the difference between the two was obvious. The temperaments that looked out from their big, dark eyes were different. The very patience of their bowed heads was different in expression. The patience of Star, the off ox, was an accepting, contented patience. Curses, blows, the jabs of the ox-goad, he took mildly, as a matter of course, and, being his master's favourite, he got just as few of them as the exigencies of backwoods ploughing and hauling would permit. But with Buck it was far otherwise. In his eyes flickered always the spark of a spirit unsubdued. He had a side glance, surly yet swift, that put the observant on their guard. He never accepted the goad without a snort of resentment, a threatening shake of his short, sharp horns. And he had command of a lightning kick which had taught discretion to more than one worrying cur. Yet he was valued, even while distrusted, by his owner, because he was intelligent, well-trained, and a glutton for work, both quicker than his docile yoke-fellow and more untiring.

Between the two great red steers there was that close attachment which has been so often observed between animals long accustomed to working in the same harness. They become a habit to each other, and seem, therefore, essential to each other's peace of mind. But on the part of Buck it was something more than this. Ill-tempered and instinctively hostile toward every one else, man or beast, he showed signs of an active devotion to his tranquil yoke-fellow, and would sometimes spend hours licking Star's neck while the latter went on chewing the cud in complacent acceptance of the attention.

The twilight gathered deeper about the lonely backwoods clearing. The night-hawk, a soaring and swooping speck in the pallid spaces of the sky, became invisible, though his strange note still twanged sonorously from time to time. The hermit hushed his fluting in the alder thicket. An owl hooted solemnly from somewhere back in the spruce woods. But still the owner of the oxen did not come to lower the bars and give admittance to the brimming trough. He was lying dead beside the brawling trout-brook, a mile or so down the tote-road, his neck broken by a flying branch from a tree which he had felled too carelessly. His dog was standing over the sprawled body, whining and pawing at it in distracted solicitude.

To the two thirsty oxen the cool smell of the waiting trough was cruelly tantalizing. To one of them it speedily became irresistible. Buck was not, by instinct, any great respecter of bounds or barriers. He began hooking impatiently at the bars, while Star gazed at him in placid wonder. The bars were solid and well set, and Buck seemed to realize almost at once that there was little to be done in that quarter. Feeling for a weak spot, he worked his way along beyond them to the first panel of the fence. It was the ordinary rough "snake" of the backwoods clearing, a zigzag structure of rough poles, supported at the angles by crossed stakes. Never very substantial, it had been broken and somewhat carelessly mended at this particular point. The top rail lifted easily under the thrust of Buck's aimlessly tossing horn. It fell down again at once into its place in the crotch of the crossed stakes, and, in falling, it struck the fumbling experimenter a sharp whack across the nose.

The hot-tempered steer, already irritated, flared up at once, and butted heavily at the fence with his massive forehead. One of the cross-stakes, already half-rotted through, broke at once, and the two top rails went down with a crash. Following up this push, he threw his ponderous weight against the remaining rails, now left unsupported, breasted them down almost without an effort, and went crashing and triumphing through into the yard. His mate, who would never himself have dreamed of such a venture as breaking bounds, stared irresolutely for a few seconds, then followed through the gap. And side by side the two slaked their thirst, plunging their broad muzzles into the cool of the trough and lifting them to blow the drops luxuriously from their nostrils.

The impulse of Star was now to turn back into the familiar pasture, according to custom. But Buck, on the other hand, was used to being driven back and that always more or less under protest. For the first time in his memory, there was now no one to drive him back. He had a strange, new sense of freedom, of restraint removed. He was accustomed to seeing a light in the cabin window about this hour. But there was no light. The whole place seemed empty with a new kind of emptiness. Nothing was further from his fancy than to return to the pasture prison which he had just broken out of. He stood with head uplifted, as if already the galling memory of the yoke had slipped from off his neck.

For a minute or two he stood sniffing with wide nostrils, drinking deep the chill, keen-scented air. It was the same air as he had been breathing on the other side of the pasture-bars, but it smelt very different to him. Something there was in it which called him away irresistibly into the dark, unfenced depths of the forest which surrounded the clearing. He turned his great head and lowed coaxingly to his partner, who was standing beside the gap in the pasture fence and staring after him in placid question. Then he started off with a brisk step down the shadowy, pale ribbon of the road.

Star's natural impulse, after drinking, was to return to the familiar, comfortable pasture; but not without his yoke-mate. The stronger impulse ruled. With some reluctance and a good deal of bovine wonder, he swung around and hastened after Buck. The latter waited for him; and side by side, as if in yoke, though with less labouring steps, they turned off the deeply rutted highway and moved silently down a mossed old wood road into the glimmering dark of the forest.

A sure instinct in Buck's feet was leading them straight away from the Settlements, straight into the heart of the wilderness. After perhaps an hour the wood-road led out of the thick forest across a little wild meadow with a shallow brook babbling softly through it. Here the two grazed for a time, almost belly deep in the thick-flowered grass, while the bats flickered and zigzagged above them, and a couple of whip-poor-wills answered each other monotonously from opposite ends of the glade. Then they lay down side by side to chew the cud and to sleep, surrounded by the pungent smell of the stalks of the wild parsnip which their huge bulks had crushed down.

They lay in a corner of the glade, close to the dense thickets that formed the fringe of the woods. Unaccustomed to vigilance, neither their eyes nor their ears were on the alert. A lynx crept up behind them, within a dozen paces, glared at them vindictively with its pale, malignant moon-eyes, and then ran up a tree to get a better look at these mighty intruders upon his hunting-ground. His claws made a loud rattling on the bark as he climbed, but neither of the oxen paid any attention whatever to the sound. Of course, a lynx could not, under any circumstances, be anything more than an object of mild curiosity to them, but had it been a pair of hungry panthers, they would have been equally unconscious and unwarned. They lay with their backs to the forest, looking out across the open, chewing lazily, and from time to time heaving windy breaths of deep content. Not a score of yards before their noses a trailing weasel ran down and killed a hare. At the cry of the victim Buck opened his half-closed eyes and gave a snort of disapproval. But Star paid no attention whatever to the little tragedy. All his faculties were engrossed upon his comfort and his cud.

A little later a prowling fox came suddenly upon them. He was surprised to find the pair so far from their pasture, where he had several times observed them in the course of his wide wanderings. His shrewd mind jumped to the idea that perhaps the settler, their master, was out with them; and while he had no objection whatever to the oxen--stupid, harmless hulks in his eyes--he had the most profound objection to their master and his gun. He slipped back into cover, encircled the whole glade stealthily till he picked up their trail, and satisfied himself that they had come alone. Then he returned and sat down on his tail deliberately in front of them, cocking his head to one side, as if inviting them to explain their presence.

Star returned his gaze with placid indifference, but Buck was annoyed. In his eyes the fox was a little sharp-nosed dog with a bushy tail and an exasperating smell. He hated all dogs, but especially little ones, because they were so elusive when they yapped at his heels. He heaved himself up with an angry snort, and charged upon the intruder. The fox, without losing his dignity at all, seemed to drift easily out of reach, to this side or that, till the ox grew tired of the futile chase. Moreover, as the fox made no sound and no demonstration of heel-snapping, Buck's anger presently faded out, and he returned to his partner's side and lay down again. And the fox, his curiosity satisfied, trotted away.

A little later there came a stealthy crashing through the darkness of the underbush in the rear. But the two oxen never turned their heads. To them the ominous sound had no significance whatever. A few paces behind them the crashing came to a sudden stop. A bear, lumbering down toward the brook-side, to grub in the soft earth for edible roots, had caught the sound of their breathing and chewing. He knew the sound, for he, too, like the fox, had prowled about the pasture fence at night. As noiselessly as a shadow he crept nearer, till he could make out the contented pair. He knew they belonged to the man, and it made him uneasy to see them there, so far from where they belonged. He sniffed the air cautiously, to see if the man was with them. No, the man was not there, that was soon obvious. He had no thought of attacking them; they were much too formidable to be meddled with. But why were they there? The circumstance was, therefore, dangerous. Perhaps the man was designing some sort of trap for him. He drew back cautiously, and made off by the way he had come. He had a wholesome respect for the man, and for all his works and belongings.

In the first, mysterious, glassy grey of dawn, when thin wisps of vapour clung curling among the grass-tops, the two wanderers got up and fell to grazing. Then Star, who was beginning to feel homesick for old pasture fields, strayed away irresolutely toward the road for home. Buck, however, would have none of it. He marched off toward the brook, splashed through, and fell to pasturing again on the farther side. Star, not enduring to be left alone, immediately joined him.

That day the pair pressed onward, deeper and deeper into the wilds, Buck ever eager on the unknown quest, Star ever reluctant, but persuaded. As a matter of fact, had Star been resolute enough in his reluctance, had he had the independence to lie down and refuse to go farther, he would have gained the day, for Buck would never have forsaken him. But initiative ruled inertia, as is usually the case, and Buck's adventuring spirit had its way.

It was a rugged land, but hospitable enough to the wanderers in this affluent late June weather, through which Buck so confidently led the way. The giant tangle of the forest was broken by frequent wild meadows, and foaming streams, and lonely little granite-bordered lakes, and stretches of sun-steeped barren, all bronze green with blueberry scrub. There was plenty to eat, plenty to drink, and when the flies and the heat grew troublesome, it was pleasant to wallow in the cold, amber-brown pools. Even Star began to forget the home pasture, and content himself with the freedom which he had never craved.

How far and to what goal the urge in Buck's untamed heart would have carried them before exhausting itself, there is no telling. But he had challenged without knowledge the old, implacable sphinx of the wilderness. And suddenly, to his undoing, the challenge was accepted.

On the third day of their wanderings the pair came out upon a river too deep and wide for even Buck's daring to attempt to cross. The banks were steep--a succession of rocky bluffs, broken by deep lateral bayous, and strips of interval meadows where brooks came in through a fringe of reeds and alders. Buck turned northward, following the bank up stream, sometimes close to the edge, sometimes a little way back, wheresoever the easier path or the most tempting patches of pasturage might seem to lead. He was searching always for some feasible crossing, for his instinct led him always to get over any barrier. That his path toward the west had been barred only confirmed him in his impulse to work westward.

Late that afternoon, as they burst out, through thick bushes, into a little grassy glade, they surprised a bear-cub playing with a big yellow fungus, which he boxed and cuffed about--carefully, so as not to break his plaything-- as a kitten boxes a ball. To Buck, of course, the playful cub was only another dog, which might be expected to come yapping and snapping at his heels. With an indignant snort he charged it.

The cub, at that ominous sound, looked up in astonishment. But when he saw the terrible red form dashing down upon him across the grass, he gave a squeal of terror and fled for the shelter of the trees. He was too young, however, for any great speed or agility, and he had none of the dog's artfulness in dodging. Before he could gain cover he was overtaken. Buck's massive front caught him on his haunches, smashing him into the ground. He gave one agonized squall, and then the life was crushed out of him.

Amazed at this easy success--the first of the kind he had ever had--but immensely proud of himself, the great red ox drew off and eyed his victim for a second or two, his tail lashing his sides in angry triumph. Then he fell to goring the small black body, and tossing it into the air, and battering it again with his forehead as it came down. He was taking deep vengeance for all the yelping curs which had worried and eluded him in the past.

In the midst of this congenial exercise he caught sight, out of the corner of his eye, of a big black shape just hurling itself upon him. The mother bear, a giant of her kind, had come to the cry of her little one.

Buck whirled with amazing nimbleness to meet the attack. He was in time to escape the blow which would have cracked even his mighty neck, but the long, steel-hard claws of his assailant fairly raked off one side of his face, destroying one eye completely. At the same time, with a shrill bellow, he lunged forward, driving a short, punishing horn deep into the bear's chest and hurling her back upon her haunches.

Dreadful as was his own injury, this fortunate thrust gave him the advantage for the moment. But, being unlearned in battle, he did not know enough to follow it up. He drew back to prepare for another charge, and paused to stamp the ground, and bellow, and shake his horribly wounded head.

The mother, heedless of her own deep wound, turned to sniff, whimpering, at the body of her cub. Seeing at once that it was quite dead, she wheeled like a flash and hurled herself again upon the slayer. As she wheeled she came upon Buck's blinded side. He lunged forward once again, mad for the struggle. But this time, half blind as he was, he was easily eluded, for the old bear was a skilled fighter. A monstrous weight crashed down upon his neck, just behind the ears, and the bright green world grew black before him. He stumbled heavily forward on knees and muzzle, with a choking bellow. The bear struck again, and with the other paw tore out his throat, falling upon him and mauling him with silent fury as he rolled over upon his side.

Star, meanwhile, being ever slow of wit and of purpose, had been watching with startled eyes, unable to take in the situation, although a strange heat was beginning to stretch his veins. But when he saw his yoke-mate stumble forward on his muzzle, when he heard that choking bellow of anguish, then the unaccustomed fire found its way up into his brain. He saw red, and, with a nimbleness far beyond that of Buck at his swiftest, he launched himself into the battle.

The bear, absorbed in the fulness of her vengeance, was taken absolutely by surprise. It was as if a ton of rock had been hurled against her flank, rolling her over and crushing her at the same time. In his rage the great red ox seemed suddenly to develop an aptitude for the battle. Twisting his head, he buried one horn deep in his adversary's belly, where he ripped and tore with the all-destructive fury of a mad rhinoceros. The bear's legs closed convulsively about his head and shoulders, but in the next instant they relaxed again, falling away loosely as that ploughing horn reached and pierced the heart. Then Star drew back, and stood shaking his head to clear the blood out of his eyes.

For two days and nights Star stood over his yoke-mate's body, leaving his post only for a few yards and for a few minutes, at long intervals, to crop a mouthful of grass or to drink at that cold stream which ran past the edge of the tragic glade. On the third day two woodsmen, passing down the river in a canoe, were surprised to hear the lowing of an ox in that desolate place, far from even the remotest settler's cabin. The lowing was persistent and appealing. They went ashore and investigated.

At the scene which they came upon in the sunny little glade they stood marvelling. After a time their shrewd conjectures, initiated as they were in all the mysteries of the wild, arrived at a fairly accurate interpretation of it all.

"It was sure some scrap, anyhow," was the final conclusion of one grizzled investigator; and "Wish't we could 'a' seen it," of the other. Then, the big red ox, with blood caked over head and horns, being too admired as well as too valuable to be left behind, they decided that one of them should stop on shore and drive him, while the other followed slowly in the canoe.

At first Star refused stolidly to budge from his dead comrade's side. But the woodsman was in winter a teamster, and what he did not know about driving oxen was not worth knowing. He cut a long white stick like an ox-goad, took his place at Star's side, gave him a firm prod in the flank, and cried in a voice of authority: "Haw, Bright!"

At the old command, although "Bright" was not the right name, Star seemed once more to feel the familiar, and to him not unpleasant, pressure of the yoke upon his neck. He swerved obediently to the left, lowering his head and throwing his weight forward to start the imaginary load, and moved away as his new master ordered. And gradually, as he went, directed this way or that by the sharp commands of "Gee!" or "Haw!" and the light reminder of the goad, his grief for his yoke-fellow began to dull its edge. It was comforting to be once more controlled, to be snatched back into servitude from a freedom which had proved so strenuous and so terrible.

The Trailers

Young Stan Murray turned on his heel and went into the house for his gun. His breast boiled with pity and indignation. The hired man, coming down from the Upper Field, had just told him that two more of his sheep had been killed by the bears. The sheep were of fine stock, only lately introduced to the out-settlements, and they were Stan's special charge. These two last made seven that the bears had taken within six weeks. Stan Murray, with the robust confidence of his eighteen years, vowed that the marauder, or marauders, should be brought to an accounting without more ado, though it should take him a week to trail them down. He stuffed some hardtack biscuits and a generous lump of cheese into his pockets, saw that his Winchester repeater was duly charged, buckled on his cartridge-belt, and started for the Upper Field.

The hired man led him to the scene of the tragedy. The two victims--both full-grown sheep--had been struck down close to the edge of the field, within a dozen yards of each other. Nothing was left of them there but their woolly skins and big sploshes of darkened blood on the stiff turf of the pasture. The carcases had evidently been dragged or carried off into the dark seclusion of the fir woods which bordered the top and farther side of the field. It was now just after midday, and Stan and the hired man agreed, after examination of all the signs, that the killing must have taken place early the previous night.

"It's a long ways from here them b'ar'll be by this time, I'm thinkin'," said the hired man. Not a native of the backwoods, he was little versed in wilderness lore.

"Not at all," corrected Murray. "Like as not they're within a half mile or so of us now. They wouldn't lug those fat sheep far. They'd just eat what they wanted an' hide the rest in the bushes. And they'd come back an' finish it up when they'd slept off the first feed. What would they want to travel for, when they'd got such a dead easy thing right here?"

"Um-m-m!" grunted the hired man grudgingly. "Mebbe you're right. But I'd like to know who's been here afore us, an' rolled up this here skin so tidy-like? T'other skin's left all of a heap, mebbe because it's so torn 'tain't no good to nobody."

The young woodsman laughed, for all his vexation of spirit.

"Lot you know about bears, Tom," said he. "You see, there's been two bears here on this job, curse their dirty hides! One's a youngster, an' don't know much about skinning a sheep. He's just clawed off the skin any old way, an' made a mess of it, as you see. But the other's an old hand, evidently, an' knows what he's about--an old she, likely, an' perhaps mother of the young one. She's known how to peel off the skin, rolling it up that way quite as a man might do. Now, Tom, you get along back home, an' take the skins with you. I'm going after those two, an' I'm not coming home till I've squared up with 'em over this here deal."

For half a mile or more back into the woods the trail of the marauders was a plain one to follow. Then Murray found the remnants of the two victims hidden in a mass of thick underbush, several yards apart. The tracks of the two bears encircled the spot, a plain proclamation of ownership to any other of the wild creatures which might be inclined to trespass on that domain. And on the trunk of a tall spruce, standing close beside the hiding-place, the initiated eyes of young Murray detected another warning to intruders. The bark at a considerable height was scored by the marks of mighty claws. The larger bear, after her meal, had stretched herself like a cat, rearing herself and digging in her claws against the trunk. And the great height of her reach was a pointed announcement that her displeasure would be a perilous thing to reckon with. As Stan Murray stood, estimating the stature of his foe, his eyes began to sparkle. This would be a trophy worth winning, the hide and head of such a bear. His wrath against the slayers of his sheep died away into the emulous zest of the hunter.

The bears, their hunger satisfied, had gone on straight back into the wilderness, instead of hanging about the scene of their triumph or crawling into a neighbouring thicket, as Murray had expected, to sleep off their heavy feast. Murray thought he knew all about bears. As a matter of fact, he did know a lot about them. What he did not know was that no one, however experienced and sympathetic an observer, ever does achieve to know all about them. The bear is at the opposite pole from the sheep. He is an individualist. He does not care to do as his neighbour does. He is ever ready to adapt his habits, as well as his diet, to the varying of circumstance. He loves to depart from his rules and confound the naturalists. When you think you've got him, he turns out to be an old black stump, and laughs in his shaggy sleeve from some other hidden post of observation. He makes all the other kindred of the wild, except, perhaps, the shrewd fox, seem like foolish children beside him.

For a good hour Murray followed the trail of the two bears, at times with some difficulty, as the forest gave way in places to breadths of hard and stony barren, where the great pads left smaller trace. At last, to his annoyance, in a patch of swamp, where the trail was very clear, he realized that he was now following one bear only, and that the smaller of the two. He cast assiduously from side to side, but in vain. He harked back along the trail for several hundred yards, but he could find no sign of the other bear, nor of where she had branched off. And it was just that other that he wanted. However, he decided that as the two were working together, he would probably find the second by keeping on after the first, rather than by questing at large for a lost trail. In any case, as he now reminded himself, it was not a trophy, but vengeance for his slaughtered sheep that he was out for.

The trail he had been following hitherto had been hours old. Now, of a sudden, he noticed with a start that it had become amazingly fresh--so fresh, indeed, that he felt he might come upon his quarry at any instant. How did it happen that the trail had thus grown fresh all at once? Decidedly puzzled, he halted abruptly and sat down upon a stump to consider the problem.

At last he came to the conclusion that, somewhere to his rear, the quarry must have swerved off to one side or the other, either lain down for a brief siesta, or made a wide detour, then circled back into the old trail just a little way in advance of him. Again, it seemed, he had overshot the important and revealing point of the trail. He was nettled, disappointed in himself. His first impulse was to retrace his steps minutely, and try to verify this conclusion. Then he reflected that, after all, he had better content himself with the fact that he was now close on the heels of the fugitive, and vengeance, perhaps, almost within his grasp. To go back, for the mere sake of proving a theory, would be to lose his advantage. Moreover, the afternoon was getting on. He decided to push forward.

But now he went warily, peering to this side and to that, and scrutinizing every thicket, every stump and massive bole. He felt that he had been too confident, and made too much noise in his going. It was pretty certain that the quarry would by now be aware of the pursuit, and cunningly on guard. Twice he had been worsted in woodcraft. He was determined that the marauders should not score off him a third time.

For another half-hour he kept on, moving now as noiselessly as a mink, and watchfully as a wood-mouse. Yet the trail went on as before, and he could detect no sign that he was gaining on the elusive quarry. At last, grown suddenly conscious of hunger, he sat down upon a mossy stone and proceeded to munch his crackers and cheese. He was getting rather out of conceit with himself, and the meal, hungry though he was, seemed tasteless.

As he sat there, gnawing discontentedly at his dry fare, he began to feel conscious of being watched. The short hairs on the back of his neck tingled and rose. He looked around sharply, but he could see nothing. Very softly he rose to his feet. With minutest scrutiny his eyes searched every object within view. The mingled shadows of the forest were confusing, of course, but his trained eyes knew how to differentiate them. Nevertheless, neither behind, nor before, nor on either side could he make out any living thing, except a little black-and-white woodpecker, which peered at him with unwinking curiosity from a gnarled trunk a dozen feet away. From the woodpecker his glance wandered upwards and interrogated the lower branches of the surrounding trees. At last he made out the gleam of a pair of pale, malevolent eyes glaring down upon him from a high branch. Then he made out the shadowy shape, flattened close to the branch, of a large wild-cat.

Murray disliked the whole tribe of the wild-cats, as voracious destroyers of game and cunning depredators upon his poultry, and his rifle went instantly to his shoulder. But he lowered it again with a short laugh. He was not bothering just then with wild-cats. He cursed himself softly as "getting nervous," and sat down again to resume his meal, satisfied that the sensation at the back of his neck was now explained.

But he had not found the true explanation, by any means. In fact, he was fooled yet again.

From less than fifty yards ahead of him a little pair of red-rimmed eyes, half angry and half curious, were watching his every movement. Crouching behind two great trunks, his quarry was keeping him under wary observation, ready to slip onward like a shadow, keeping to the shelter of the thicket and bole and rock, the moment he should show the least sign of taking up the trail again.

Moreover, from a slightly greater distance to his rear, another pair of little red-rimmed eyes, less curious and more angry, also held him under observation. For an hour or more, at least, the older bear had been trailing him in her turn with practised cunning. For all her immense bulk, she had never betrayed herself by so much as the crackling of a twig; and the unconscious, complacent hunter was being hunted with a woodcraft far beyond his own. Whenever he stopped, or paused for the least moment, she came to a stop herself as instantly as if worked by the same nerve impulse, and stiffened into such stony immobility that she seemed at once to melt into her surroundings, and became invisible in the sense of being indistinguishable from them. Among mossy rocks she seemed to become a rock, among stumps a stump, among thickets a portion of the dark, shaggy undergrowth.

Having finished his crackers and cheese, Murray got up, brushed the crumbs from his jacket, flicked a hard flake of bark contemptuously at the wild-cat--which darted farther up the tree with an angry growl--and once more took up the trail. He was beginning now to wonder if he was going to accomplish anything before the light should fail him, and he hurried on at a swifter pace. A few hundred yards farther, to his considerable gratification, the trail swept around in a wide curve towards the right, and made back towards the Settlement. "Perhaps," he thought, "that fool of a bear does not know, after all, that I am on his track, and is going back for the remainder of his supper."

Encouraged by this idea, he pushed on faster still.

Then, some ten minutes later, he had reason to regret his haste. Crossing a patch of soft, open ground, his attention was caught by the fact that the footprints he was following had miraculously increased in size. Examination proved that this was no illusion. And now, for the first time, an unpleasant feeling crept over him. Apparently he was being played with. The second bear, it was evident, had slipped in and taken the place of the first, copying an old game of the hunted foxes.

Murray suddenly felt himself alone and outwitted. If it had been earlier in the day, he would not have cared; but now it would soon be night. He had no great dread of bears, as a rule. He was willing to tackle several of them at once, as long as he had his Winchester and a clear chance to use it--but after dark he would be at a grievous disadvantage. If the trail had still been leading away from home, he would probably have turned back and planned for an early start again next morning. But as his enemy was going in the right direction, he decided to follow on as fast as possible, and see if he might not succeed in obtaining a decision before dark.

The trail was now almost insolently clear, and he followed it at a lope. He gained no glimpse of the quarry even at this pace; but at least he had the satisfaction of knowing, from the increased heaviness of the footprints and the lengthening of the stride, that he was forcing his adversary to make haste. Presently it appeared that this was displeasing to the adversary. The trail went off to the left, at a sharp angle, and made for a dense cedar swamp, which Murray had no desire to adventure into at that late hour. He decided to give up the chase for the day and keep straight for home.

By this time Murray felt that his knowledge of bears was not quite so profound as he had fancied it to be. Nevertheless, he was sure of one thing. He was ready to gamble on it that, as soon as they realized he had given up trailing them, they would turn and trail him. The idea was more or less depressing to him in his present mood. He did not greatly care, however, so long as it was fairly light. He did not think that his adversaries would have the rashness to attack him even after dark, the black bear having a very just appreciation of man's power. Still, there was the chance, and it gave him something to think of. He made a hurried estimate of the distance he had yet to go, and it was with a distinct sense of relief he concluded that he would make the open fields before the closing in of dark.

The woods at this point were somewhat thick, an abundant second growth of spruce and fir. Presently they fell away before him, revealing a few acres of windy grass-land surrounding a deserted cabin. At the sight of the space of open ground Murray was seized with a new idea. His face brightened, his self-confidence returned. The bears had, so far, outdone him thoroughly in woodcraft. Well, he would now show them that he was their master in tactics.

He ran staggeringly out into the field, and fell as if exhausted. He lay for a few seconds, to make sure he was observed by his antagonists, then picked himself up, raced on across the open as fast as he could, and plunged into the thick woods on the opposite side.

As soon as he was hidden, he turned and looked behind him. The growth of bushes and rank herbage which fringed the other side of the clearing whence he had come was waving and tossing with the movement of heavy bodies.

For a few moments he thought that his pursuers, grown bold with his flight, would break forth from their concealment and follow across the clearing. In that case he might count on bagging them both.

But no, they were too wary still for that. Presently the tossing of the bushes began to separate, and moved rapidly both to right and left along the skirts of the clearing. A smile of triumph spread over Murray's face.

"My turn at last!" he muttered, and ran noiselessly, keeping well hidden, down toward the left-hand corner of the field. He had an idea that it was the bigger bear which was coming to meet him in that direction, because the movement of the bushes had seemed the more violent on that side. He was himself again fully now, the zest of the hunter swallowing up all other emotions.

Just at the corner of the field, behind a heap of stones half buried in herbage, he hid himself, and lay motionless, with his rifle at his shoulder and finger on the trigger. He could hear the bear coming, for she was running more carelessly now, under the impression that the enemy was in full flight. Dry branches snapped, green branches swished and rustled, and occasionally his straining ears caught the sound of a heavy but muffled footfall.

She was almost upon him, however, before he could actually get a view of her. She came out into a space between two clumps of young fir trees, not twenty-five yards from his hiding-place, and was just passing him diagonally, offering a perfect mark. Murray's finger closed, softly and steadily, on the trigger. The heavy, soft-nosed bullet crashed through her neck, and she dropped, collapsing on the instant into nothing more than a heap of rusty-black fur.

Immensely elated, his dear sheep avenged, and his standing as a hunter vindicated at last, young Murray strode over and examined his splendid prize. It was by far the biggest black bear he had ever seen. To the other of the pair he gave not a thought; he knew that the crack of his rifle would have cured it of any further curiosity it might have had about himself. He took out his handkerchief, tied it to the end of a stick, and stuck the stick into the ground beside the heap of fur, to serve both as a mark and as a warning to possible trespassers. Then he made haste home, to fetch a lantern and the hired man, for he would not leave so splendid a skin all night to the mercies of fox and fisher and weasel and other foragers of the dark.

Cock-Crow

He was a splendid bird, a thoroughbred "Black-breasted Red" game-cock, his gorgeous plumage hard as mail, silken with perfect condition, and glowing like a flame against the darkness of the spruce forest. His snaky head--the comb and wattles had been trimmed close, after the mode laid down for his aristocratic kind--was sharp and keen, like a living spear-point. His eyes were fierce and piercing, ready ever to meet the gaze of bird, or beast, or man himself, with the unwinking challenge of their full, arrogant stare.

Perched upon a stump a few yards from the railway line, he turned that bold stare now, with an air of unperturbed superciliousness, upon the wreck of the big freight-car from which he had just escaped. He had escaped by a miracle, but little effect had that upon his bold and confident spirit. The ramshackle, overladen freight train, labouring up the too-steep gradient, had broken in two, thanks to a defective coupler, near the top of the incline a mile and a half away. The rear cars--heavy box-cars--had, of course, run back, gathering a terrific momentum as they went. The rear brakeman, his brakes failing to hold, had discreetly jumped before the speed became too great. At the foot of the incline a sharp curve had proved too much for the runaways to negotiate. With a screech of tortured metal they had jumped the track, and gone crashing down the high embankment. One car, landing on a granite boulder, had split apart like a cleft melon. The light crate in which our game-cock, a pedigree bird, was being carried to a fancier in the nearest town, some three score miles away, had survived by its very lightness. But its door had been snapped open. The cock walked out deliberately, uttered a long, low krr-rr-ee of ironic comment upon the disturbance, hopped delicately over the tangle of boxes and crates and agricultural implements, and flew to the top of the nearest stump. There he shook himself, his plumage being disarrayed, though his spirit was not. He flapped his wings. Then, eyeing the wreckage keenly, he gave a shrill, triumphant crow, which rang through the early morning stillness of the forest like a challenge. He felt that the smashed car, so lately his prison, was a foe which he had vanquished by his own unaided prowess. His pride was not altogether unnatural.

The place where he stood preening the red glory of his plumage was in the very heart of the wilderness. The only human habitation within a dozen miles in either direction was a section-man's shanty, guarding a siding and a rusty water-tank. The woods--mostly spruce in that region, with patches of birch and poplar--had been gone over by the lumbermen some five years before, and still showed the ravages of the insatiable axe. Their narrow "tote-roads," now deeply mossed and partly overgrown by small scrub, traversed the lonely spaces in every direction. One of these roads led straight back into the wilderness from the railway--almost from the stump whereon the red cock had his perch.

The cock had no particular liking for the neighbourhood of the accident, and when his fierce, inquiring eye fell upon this road, he decided to investigate, hoping it might lead him to some flock of his own kind, over whom he would, as a matter of course, promptly establish his domination. That there would be other cocks there, already in charge, only added to his zest for the adventure. He was raising his wings to hop down from his perch, when a wide-winged shadow passed over him, and he checked himself, glancing upwards sharply.

A foraging hawk had just flown overhead. The hawk had never before seen a bird like the bright figure standing on the stump, and he paused in his flight, hanging for a moment on motionless wing to scrutinise the strange apparition. But he was hungry, and he considered himself more than a match for anything in feathers except the eagle, the goshawk, and the great horned owl. His hesitation was but for a second, and, with a sudden mighty thrust of his wide wings, he swooped down upon this novel victim.

The big hawk was accustomed to seeing every quarry he stooped at cower paralysed with terror or scurry for shelter in wild panic. But, to his surprise, this infatuated bird on the stump stood awaiting him, with wings half lifted, neck feathers raised in a defiant ruff, and one eye cocked upwards warily. He was so surprised, in fact, that at a distance of some dozen or fifteen feet he wavered and paused in his downward rush. But it was surprise only, fear having small place in his wild, marauding heart. In the next second he swooped again and struck downwards at his quarry with savage, steel-hard talons.

He struck but empty air. At exactly the right fraction of the instant the cock had leapt upwards on his powerful wings, lightly as a thistle-seed, but swift as if shot from a catapult. He passed straight over his terrible assailant's back. In passing he struck downwards with his spurs, which were nearly three inches long, straight, and tapered almost to a needle-point. One of these deadly weapons found its mark, as luck would have it, fair in the joint of the hawk's shoulder, putting the wing clean out of action.

The marauder turned completely over and fell in a wild flutter to the ground, the cock, at the same time, alighting gracefully six or eight feet away and wheeling like a flash to meet a second attack. The hawk, recovering with splendid nerve from the amazing shock of his overthrow, braced himself upright on his tail by the aid of the one sound wing--the other wing trailing helplessly--and faced his strange adversary with open beak and one clutching talon uplifted.

The cock, fighting after the manner of his kind, rushed in to within a couple of feet of his foe and there paused, balanced for the next stroke or parry, legs slightly apart, wings lightly raised, neck feathers ruffed straight out, beak lowered and presented like a rapier point. Seeing that his opponent made no demonstration, but simply waited, watching him with eyes as hard and bright and dauntless as his own, he tried to provoke him to a second attack. With scornful insolence he dropped his guard and pecked at a twig or a grass blade, jerking the unconsidered morsel aside and presenting his point again with lightning swiftness.

The insult, however, was lost upon the hawk, who had no knowledge of the cock's duelling code. He simply waited, motionless as the stump beside him.

[Illustration: Leaping upwards and striking downwards with his destroying heels.]

The cock, perceiving that taunt and insolence were wasted, now began to circle warily toward the left, as if to take his opponent in the flank. The hawk at once shifted front to face him. But this was the side of his disabled wing. The sprawling member would not move, would not get out of the way. In the effort to manage it, he partly lost his precarious balance. The cock saw his advantage instantly. He dashed in like a feathered and flaming thunderbolt, leaping upwards and striking downwards with his destroying heels. The hawk was hurled over backwards, with one spur through his throat, the other through his lungs. As he fell he dragged his conqueror down with him, and one convulsive but blindly-clutching talon ripped away a strip of flesh and feathers from the victor's thigh. There was a moment's flapping, a few delicate red feathers floated off upon the morning air, then the hawk lay quite still, and the red cock, stepping haughtily off the body of his foe, crowed long and shrill, three times, as if challenging any other champions of the wilderness to come and dare a like fate.

For a few minutes he stood waiting and listening for an answer to his challenge. As no answer came, he turned, without deigning to glance at his slain foe, and stalked off, stepping daintily, up the old wood-road and into the depths of the forest. To the raw, red gash in his thigh he paid no heed whatever.

Having no inkling of the fact that the wilderness, silent and deserted though it seemed, was full of hostile eyes and unknown perils, he took no care at all for the secrecy of his going. Indeed, had he striven for concealment, his brilliant colouring, so out of key with the forest gloom, would have made it almost impossible. Nevertheless, his keenness of sight and hearing, his practised and unsleeping vigilance as protector of his flock, stood him in good stead, and made up for his lack of wilderness lore. It was with an intense interest and curiosity, rather than with any apprehension, that his bold eyes questioned everything on either side of his path through the dark spruce woods. Sometimes he would stop to peck the bright vermilion bunches of the pigeon-berry, which here and there starred the hillocks beside the road. But no matter how interesting he found the novel and delicious fare, his vigilance never relaxed. It was, indeed, almost automatic. The idea lurking in his subconscious processes was probably that he might at any moment be seen by some doughty rival of his own kind, and challenged to the great game of mortal combat. But whatever the object of his watchfulness, it served him as well against the unknown as it could have done against expected foes.

Presently he came to a spot where an old, half-rotted stump had been torn apart by a bear hunting for wood-ants. The raw earth about the up-torn roots tempted the wanderer to scratch for grubs. Finding a fat white morsel, much too dainty to be devoured alone, he stood over it and began to call kt-kt-kt, kt-kt-kt, kt-kt-kt in his most alluring tones, hoping that some coy young hen would come stealing out of the underbrush in response to his gallant invitation. There was no such response; but as he peered about hopefully, he caught sight of a sinister, reddish-yellow shape creeping towards him behind the shelter of a withe-wood bush. He gulped down the fat grub, and stood warily eyeing the approach of this new foe.

It looked to him like a sharp-nosed, bushy-tailed yellow dog--a very savage and active one. He was not afraid, but he knew himself no match for a thoroughly ferocious dog of that size. This one, it was clear, had evil designs upon him. He half crouched, with wings loosed and every muscle tense for the spring.

The next instant the fox pounced at him, darting through the green edges of the withe-wood bush with most disconcerting suddenness. The cock sprang into the air, but only just in time, for the fox, leaping up nimbly at him with snapping jaws, captured a mouthful of glossy tail feathers. The cock alighted on a branch overhead, some seven or eight feet from the ground, whipped around, stretched his neck downwards, and eyed his assailant with a glassy stare. "Kr-rr-rr-eee?" he murmured softly, as if in sarcastic interrogation. The fox, exasperated at his failure, and hating, above all beasts, to be made a fool of, glanced around to see if there were any spectators. Then, with an air of elaborate indifference, he pawed a feather from the corner of his mouth and trotted away as if he had just remembered something.

He had not gone above thirty yards or so, when the cock flew down again to the exact spot where he had been scratching. He pretended to pick up another grub, all the time keeping an eye on the retiring foe. He crowed with studied insolence; but the fox, although that long and shrill defiance must have seemed a startling novelty, gave no sign of having heard it. The cock crowed again, with the same lack of result. He kept on crowing until the fox was out of sight. Then he returned coolly to his scratching. When he had satisfied his appetite for fat white grubs, he flew up again to his safe perch and fell to pruning his feathers. Five minutes later the fox reappeared, creeping up with infinite stealth from quite another direction. The cock, however, detected his approach at once, and proclaimed the fact with another mocking crow. Disgusted and abashed, the fox turned in his tracks and crept away to stalk some less sophisticated quarry.

The wanderer, for all his fearlessness, was wise. He suspected that the vicious yellow dog with the bushy tail might return yet again to the charge. For a time, therefore, he sat on his perch, digesting his meal and studying with keen, inquisitive eyes his strange surroundings. After ten minutes or so of stillness and emptiness, the forest began to come alive. He saw a pair of black-and-white woodpeckers running up and down the trunk of a half-dead tree, and listened with tense interest to their loud rat-tat-tattings. He watched the shy wood-mice come out from their snug holes under the tree-roots, and play about with timorous gaiety and light rustlings among the dead leaves. He scrutinised with appraising care a big brown rabbit which came bounding in a leisurely fashion down the tote-road and sat up on his hindquarters near the stump, staring about with its mild, bulging eyes, and waving its long ears this way and that, to question every minutest wilderness sound; and he decided that the rabbit, for all its bulk and apparent vigour of limb, would not be a dangerous opponent. In fact, he thought of hopping down from his perch and putting the big innocent to flight, just to compensate himself for having had to flee from the fox.

But while he was meditating this venture, the rabbit went suddenly leaping off at a tremendous pace, evidently in great alarm. A few seconds later a slim little light-brownish creature, with short legs, long, sinuous body, short, triangular head, and cruel eyes that glowed like fire, came into view, following hard upon the rabbit's trail. It was nothing like half the rabbit's size, but the interested watcher on the branch overhead understood at once the rabbit's terror. He had never seen a weasel before, but he knew that the sinuous little beast with the eyes of death would be as dangerous almost as the fox. He noted that here was another enemy to look out for--to be avoided, if possible, to be fought with the utmost wariness if fighting should be forced upon him.

Not long after the weasel had vanished, the cock grew tired of waiting, and restless to renew the quest for the flock on which his dreams were set. He started by flying from tree to tree, still keeping along the course of the tote-road. But after he had covered perhaps a half-mile in this laborious fashion, he gave it up and hopped down again into the road. Here he went now with new caution, but with the same old arrogance of eye and bearing. He went quickly, however, for the gloom of the spruce wood had grown oppressive to him, and he wanted open fields and the unrestricted sun.

He had not gone far when he caught sight of a curious-looking animal advancing slowly down the path to meet him. It was nearly as big as the rabbit, but low on the legs; and instead of leaping along, it crawled with a certain heavy deliberation. Its colour was a dingy, greyish black-and-white, and its short black head was crowned with what looked like a heavy iron-grey pompadour brushed well back. The cock stood still, eyeing its approach suspiciously. It did not look capable of any very swift demonstration, but he was on his guard.

When it had come within three or four yards of him, he said "Kr-rr-rr-eee!" sharply, just to see what it would do, at the same time lowering his snaky head and ruffing out his neck feathers in challenge. The stranger seemed then to notice him for the first time, and instantly, to the cock's vast surprise, it enlarged itself to fully twice its previous size. Its fur, which was now seen to be quills rather than fur, stood up straight on end all over its head and body, and the quills were two or three inches in length. At this amazing spectacle the cock involuntarily backed away several paces. The stranger came straight on, however, without hastening his deliberate steps one jot. The cock waited, maintaining his attitude of challenge, till not more than three or four feet separated him from the incomprehensible apparition. Then he sprang lightly over it and turned in a flash, expecting the stranger to turn also and again confront him. The stranger, however, did nothing of the kind, but simply continued stolidly on his way, not even troubling to look round. Such stolidity was more than the cock could understand, having never encountered a porcupine before. He stared after it for some moments. Then he crowed scornfully, turned about, and resumed his lonely quest.

A little further on, to his great delight, he came out into a small clearing with a log cabin in the centre of it. A house! It was associated in his mind with an admiring, devoted flock of hens, and rivals to be ignominiously routed, and harmless necessary humans whose business it was to supply unlimited food. He rushed forward eagerly, careless as to whether he should encounter love or war.

Alas, the cabin was deserted! Even to his inexperienced eye it was long deserted. The door hung on one hinge, half open. The one small window had no glass in it. Untrodden weeds grew among the rotting chips up to and across the threshold. The roof--a rough affair of poles and bark--sagged in the middle, just ready to fall in at the smallest provocation. A red squirrel, his tail carried jauntily over his back, sat on the topmost peak of it and shrilled high derision at the wanderer as he approached.

The cock was acquainted with squirrels, and thought less than nothing of them. Ignoring the loud chatter, he tip-toed around the cabin, dejected but still inquisitive. Returning at length to the doorway, he peered in, craning his neck and uttering a low kr-rr. Finally, with head held high, he stalked in. The place was empty, save for a long bench with a broken leg and a joint of rust-eaten stove-pipe. Along two of the walls ran a double tier of bunks, in which the lumbermen had formerly slept. The cock stalked all around the place, prying in every corner and murmuring softly to himself. At last he flew up to the highest bunk, perched upon the edge of it, flapped his wings, and crowed repeatedly, as if announcing to the wilderness at large that he had taken possession. This ceremony accomplished, he flew down again, stalked out into the sunlight, and fell to scratching among the chips with an air of assured possession. And all the while the red squirrel kept on hurling shrill, unheeded abuse at him, resenting him as an intruder in the wilds.

Whenever the cock found a particularly choice grub or worm or beetle, he would hold it aloft in his beak, then lay it down and call loudly kt-kt-kt-kt-kt-kt, as if hoping thus to lure some flock of hens to the fair domain which he had seized. He had now dropped his quest, and was trusting that his subjects would come to him. That afternoon his valiant calls caught the ear of a weasel--possibly the very one which he had seen in the morning trailing the panic-stricken rabbit. The weasel came rushing upon him at once, too ferocious in its blood-lust for any such emotions as surprise or curiosity, and expecting an easy conquest. The cock saw it coming, and knew well the danger. But he was now on his own ground, responsible for the protection of an imaginary flock. He faced the peril unwavering. Fortunately for him, the weasel had no idea whatever of a fighting-cock's method of warfare. When the cock evaded the deadly rush by leaping straight at it and over it, instead of dodging aside or turning tail, the weasel was nonplussed for just a fraction of a second, and stood snarling. In that instant of hesitation the cock's keen spur struck it fairly behind the ear, and drove clean into the brain. The murderous little beast stiffened out, rolled gently over upon its side, and lay there with the soundless snarl fixed upon its half-opened jaws. Surprised at such an easy victory, the cock spurred the carcase again, just to make sure of it. Then he kicked it to one side, crowed, of course, and stared around wistfully for some appreciation of his triumph. He could not know with what changed eyes the squirrel--who feared weasels more than anything else on earth--was now regarding him.

The killing of so redoubtable an adversary as the weasel must have become known, in some mysterious fashion, for thenceforward no more of the small marauders of the forest ventured to challenge the new lordship of the clearing. For a week the cock ruled his solitude unquestioned, very lonely, but sleeplessly alert, and ever hoping that followers of his own kind would come to him from somewhere. In time, doubtless, his loneliness would have driven him forth again upon his quest; but Fate had other things in store for him.

Late one afternoon a grizzled woodsman in grey homespun, and carrying a bundle swung from the axe over his shoulder, came striding up to the cabin. The cock, pleased to see a human being once more, stalked forth from the cabin door to meet him. The woodsman was surprised at the sight of what he called a "reel barn-yard rooster" away off here in the wilds, but he was too tired and hungry to consider the question carefully. His first thought was that there would be a pleasant addition to his supper of bacon and biscuits. He dropped his axe and bundle, and made a swift grab at the unsuspecting bird. The latter dodged cleverly, ruffed his neck feathers with an angry kr-rr-rr, hopped up, and spurred the offending hand severely.

The woodsman straightened himself up, taken by surprise, and sheepishly shook the blood from his hand.

"Well, I'll be damned!" he muttered, eyeing the intrepid cock with admiration. "You're some rooster, you are! I guess you're all right. Guess I deserved that, for thinkin' of wringin' the neck o' sech a handsome an' gritty bird as you, an' me with plenty o' good bacon in me pack. Guess we'll call it square, eh?"

He felt in his pocket for some scraps of biscuits, and tossed them to the cock, who picked them up greedily and then strutted around him, plainly begging for more. The biscuit was a delightful change after an unvarying diet of grubs and grass. Thereafter he followed his visitor about like his shadow, not with servility, of course, but with a certain condescending arrogance which the woodsman found hugely amusing.

Just outside the cabin door the woodsman lit a fire to cook his evening rasher and brew his tin of tea. The cock supped with him, striding with dignity to pick up the scraps which were thrown to him, and then resuming his place at the other side of the fire. By the time the man was done, dusk had fallen; and the cock, chuckling contentedly in his throat, tip-toed into the cabin, flew up to the top bunk, and settled himself on his perch for the night. He had always been taught to expect benefits from men, and he felt that this big stranger who had fed him so generously would find him a flock to preside over on the morrow.

After a long smoke beside his dying fire, till the moon came up above the ghostly solitude, the woodsman turned in to sleep in one of the lower bunks, opposite to where the cock was roosting. He had heaped an armful of bracken and spruce branches into the bunk before spreading his blanket. And he slept very soundly.

Even the most experienced of woodsmen may make a slip at times. This one, this time, had forgotten to make quite sure that his fire was out. There was no wind when he went to bed, but soon afterwards a wind arose, blowing steadily toward the cabin. It blew the darkened embers to a glow, and little, harmless-looking flames began eating their way over the top layer of tinder-dry chips to the equally dry wall of the cabin.

* * * * *

The cock was awakened by a bright light in his eyes. A fiery glow, beyond the reddest of sunrises, was flooding the cabin. Long tongues of flame were licking about the doorway. He crowed valiantly, to greet this splendid, blazing dawn. He crowed again and yet again, because he was anxious and disturbed. As a sunrise, this one did not act at all according to precedent.

The piercing notes aroused the man, who was sleeping heavily. In one instant he was out of his bunk and grabbing up his blanket and his pack. In the next he had plunged out through the flaming doorway, and thrown down his armful at a safe distance, cursing acidly at such a disturbance to the most comfortable rest he had enjoyed for a week.

From within the doomed cabin came once more the crow of the cock, shrilling dauntlessly above the crackle and venomous hiss of the flames.

"Gee whizz!" muttered the woodsman, or, rather, that may be taken as the polite equivalent of his untrammelled backwoods expletive. "That there red rooster's game. Ye can't leave a pardner like that to roast!"

With one arm shielding his face, he dashed in again, grabbed the cock by the legs, and darted forth once more into the sweet, chill air, none the worse except for frizzled eyelashes and an unceremonious trimming of hair and beard. The cock, highly insulted, was flapping and pecking savagely, but the man soon reduced him to impotence, if not submission, holding him under one elbow while he tied his armed heels together, and then swaddling him securely in his coat.

"There," said he, "I guess we'll travel together from this out, pardner. Ye've sure saved my life; an' to think I had the notion, for a minnit, o' makin' a meal offen ye! I'll give ye a good home, anyways, an' I guess ye'll lick the socks offen every other rooster in the whole blame Settlement!"

The Ledge on Bald Face

That one stark naked side of the mountain which gave it its name of Old Bald Face fronted full south. Scorched by sun and scourged by storm throughout the centuries, it was bleached to an ashen pallor that gleamed startlingly across the leagues of sombre, green-purple wilderness outspread below. From the base of the tremendous bald steep stretched off the interminable leagues of cedar swamp, only to be traversed in dry weather or in frost. All the region behind the mountain face was an impenetrable jumble of gorges, pinnacles, and chasms, with black woods clinging in crevice and ravine and struggling up desperately towards the light.

In the time of spring and autumn floods, when the cedar swamps were impenetrable to all save mink, otter, and musk-rat, the only way from the western plateau to the group of lakes that formed the source of the Ottanoonsis, on the east, was by a high, nerve-testing trail across the wind-swept brow of Old Bald Face. The trail followed a curious ledge, sometimes wide enough to have accommodated an ox-wagon, at other times so narrow and so perilous that even the sure-eyed caribou went warily in traversing it.

The only inhabitants of Bald Face were the eagles, three pairs of them, who had their nests, widely separated from each other in haughty isolation, on jutting shoulders and pinnacles accessible to no one without wings. Though the ledge-path at its highest point was far above the nests, and commanded a clear view of one of them, the eagles had learned to know that those who traversed the pass were not troubling themselves about eagles' nests. They had also observed another thing--of interest to them only because their keen eyes and suspicious brains were wont to note and consider everything that came within their purview--and that was that the scanty traffic by the pass had its more or less regular times and seasons. In seasons of drought or hard frost it vanished altogether. In seasons of flood it increased the longer the floods lasted. And whenever there was any passing at all, the movement was from east to west in the morning, from west to east in the afternoon.

This fact may have been due to some sort of dimly recognised convention among the wild kindreds, arrived at in some subtle way to avoid unnecessary--and necessarily deadly--misunderstanding and struggle. For the creatures of the wild seldom fight for fighting's sake. They fight for food, or, in the mating season, they fight in order that the best and strongest may carry off the prizes.

But mere purposeless risk and slaughter they instinctively strive to avoid. The airy ledge across Bald Face, therefore, was not a place where the boldest of the wild kindred--the bear or the bull-moose, to say nothing of lesser champions--would wilfully invite the doubtful combat. If, therefore, it had been somehow arrived at that there should be no disastrous meetings, no face-to-face struggles for the right of way, at a spot where dreadful death was inevitable for one or both of the combatants, that would have been in no way inconsistent with the accepted laws and customs of the wilderness. On the other hand, it is possible that this alternate easterly and westerly drift of the wild creatures--a scanty affair enough at best of times--across the front of Bald Face was determined in the first place, on clear days, by their desire not to have the sun in their eyes in making the difficult passage, and afterwards hardened into custom. It was certainly better to have the sun behind one in treading the knife-edge pass above the eagles.

Joe Peddler found it troublesome enough, that strong, searching glare from the unclouded sun of early morning full in his eyes, as he worked over toward the Ottanoonsis lakes. He had never attempted the crossing of Old Bald Face before, and he had always regarded with some scorn the stories told by Indians of the perils of that passage. But already, though he had accomplished but a small portion of his journey, and was still far from the worst of the pass, he had been forced to the conclusion that report had not exaggerated the difficulties of his venture. However, he was steady of head and sure of foot, and the higher he went in that exquisitely clear, crisp air, the more pleased he felt with himself. His great lungs drank deep of the tonic wind which surged against him rhythmically, and seemed to him to come unbroken from the outermost edges of the world. His eyes widened and filled themselves, even as his lungs, with the ample panorama that unfolded before them. He imagined--for the woodsman, dwelling so much alone, is apt to indulge some strange imaginings--that he could feel his very spirit enlarging, as if to take full measure of these splendid breadths of sunlit, wind-washed space.

Presently, with a pleasant thrill, he observed that just ahead of him the ledge went round an abrupt shoulder of the rock-face at a point where there was a practically sheer drop of many hundreds of feet into what appeared a feather-soft carpet of tree-tops. He looked shrewdly to the security of his footing as he approached, and also to the roughnesses of the rock above the ledge, in case a sudden violent gust should chance to assail him just at the turn. He felt that at such a spot it would be so easy--indeed, quite natural--to be whisked off by the sportive wind, whirled out into space, and dropped into that green carpet so far below.

In his flexible oil-tanned "larrigans" of thick cowhide, Peddler moved noiselessly as a wild-cat, even over the bare stone of the ledge. He was like a grey shadow drifting slowly across the bleached face of the precipice. As he drew near the bend of the trail, of which not more than eight or ten paces were now visible to him, he felt every nerve grow tense with exhilarating expectation. Yet, even so, what happened was the utterly unexpected.

Around the bend before him, stepping daintily on her fine hooves, came a young doe. She completely blocked the trail just on that dizzy edge.

Peddler stopped short, tried to squeeze himself to the rock like a limpet, and clutched with fingers of iron at a tiny projection.

The doe, for one second, seemed petrified with amazement. It was contrary to all tradition that she should be confronted on that trail. Then, her amazement instantly dissolving into sheer madness of panic, she wheeled about violently to flee. But there was no room for even her lithe body to make the turn. The inexorable rock-face bounced her off, and with an agonised bleat, legs sprawling and great eyes starting from their sockets, she went sailing down into the abyss.

With a heart thumping in sympathy, Peddler leaned outward and followed that dreadful flight, till she reached that treacherously soft-looking carpet of tree-tops and was engulfed by it. A muffled crash came up to Peddler's ears.

"Poor leetle beggar!" he muttered. "I wish't I hadn't scared her so. But I'd a sight rather it was her than me!"

Peddler's exhilaration was now considerably damped. He crept cautiously to the dizzy turn of the ledge and peered around. The thought upon which his brain dwelt with unpleasant insistence was that if it had been a surly old bull-moose or a bear which had confronted him so unexpectedly, instead of that nervous little doe, he might now be lying beneath that deceitful green carpet in a state of dilapidation which he did not care to contemplate.

Beyond the turn the trail was clear to his view for perhaps a couple of hundred yards. It climbed steeply through a deep re-entrant, a mighty perpendicular corrugation of the rock-face, and then disappeared again around another jutting bastion. He hurried on rather feverishly, not liking that second interruption to his view, and regretting, for the first time, that he had no weapon with him but his long hunting-knife. He had left his rifle behind him as a useless burden to his climbing. No game was now in season, no skins in condition to be worth the shooting, and he had food enough for the journey in his light pack. He had not contemplated the possibility of any beast, even bear or bull-moose, daring to face him, because he knew that, except in mating-time, the boldest of them would give a man wide berth. But, as he now reflected, here on this narrow ledge even a buck or a lynx would become dangerous, finding itself suddenly at bay.

The steepness of the rise in the trail at this point almost drove Peddler to helping himself with his hands. As he neared the next turn, he was surprised to note, far out to his right, a soaring eagle, perhaps a hundred feet below him. He was surprised, too, by the fact that the eagle was paying no attention to him whatever, in spite of his invasion of the great bird's aerial domain. Instinctively he inferred that the eagle's nest must be in some quite inaccessible spot at safe distance from the ledge. He paused to observe from above, and thus fairly near at hand, the slow flapping of those wide wings, as they employed the wind to serve the majesty of their flight. While he was studying this, another deduction from the bird's indifference to his presence flashed upon his mind. There must be a fairly abundant traffic of the wild creatures across this pass, or the eagle would not be so indifferent to his presence. At this thought he lost his interest in problems of flight, and hurried forward again, anxious to see what might be beyond the next turn of the trail.

His curiosity was gratified all too abruptly for his satisfaction. He reached the turn, craned his head around it, and came face to face with an immense black bear.

The bear was not a dozen feet away. At sight of Peddler's gaunt dark face and sharp blue eyes appearing thus abruptly and without visible support around the rock, he shrank back upon his haunches with a startled "woof."

As for Peddler, he was equally startled, but he had too much discretion and self-control to show it. Never moving a muscle, and keeping his body out of sight so that his face seemed to be suspended in mid-air, he held the great beast's eyes with a calm, unwinking gaze.

The bear was plainly disconcerted. After a few seconds he glanced back over his shoulder, and seemed to contemplate a strategic movement to the rear. As the ledge at this point was sufficiently wide for him to turn with due care, Peddler expected now to see him do so. But what Peddler did not know was that dim but cogent "law of the ledge," which forbade all those who travelled by it to turn and retrace their steps, or to pass in the wrong direction at the wrong time. He did not know what the bear knew namely--that if that perturbed beast should turn, he was sure to be met and opposed by other wayfarers, and thus to find himself caught between two fires.

Watching steadily, Peddler was unpleasantly surprised to see the perturbation in the bear's eyes slowly change into a savage resentment-- resentment at being baulked in his inalienable right to an unopposed passage over the ledge. To the bear's mind that grim, confronting face was a violation of the law which he himself obeyed loyally and without question. To be sure, it was the face of man, and therefore to be dreaded. It was also mysterious, and therefore still more to be dreaded. But the sense of bitter injustice, with the realisation that he was at bay and taken at a disadvantage, filled him with a frightened rage which swamped all other emotion. Then he came on.

His advance was slow and cautious by reason of the difficulty of the path and his dread lest that staring, motionless face should pounce upon him just at the perilous turn and hurl him over the brink. But Peddler knew that his bluff was called, and that his only chance was to avoid the encounter. He might have fled by the way he had come, knowing that he would have every advantage in speed on that narrow trail. But before venturing up to the turn he had noted a number of little projections and crevices in the perpendicular wall above him. Clutching at them with fingers of steel and unerring toes, he swarmed upwards as nimbly as a climbing cat. He was a dozen feet up before the bear came crawling and peering around the turn.

Elated at having so well extricated himself from so dubious a situation, Peddler gazed down upon his opponent and laughed mockingly. The sound of that confident laughter from straight above his head seemed to daunt the bear and thoroughly damp his rage. He crouched low, and scurried past growling. As he hurried along the trail at a rash pace, he kept casting anxious glances over his shoulder, as if he feared the man were going to chase him. Peddler lowered himself from his friendly perch and continued his journey, cursing himself more than ever for having been such a fool as not to bring his rifle.

In the course of the next half-hour he gained the highest point of the ledge, which here was so broken and precarious that he had little attention to spare for the unparalleled sweep and splendour of the view. He was conscious, however, all the time, of the whirling eagles, now far below him, and his veins thrilled with intense exhilaration. His apprehensions had all vanished under the stimulus of that tonic atmosphere. He was on the constant watch, however, scanning not only the trail ahead--which was now never visible for more than a hundred yards or so at a time--and also the face of the rock above him, to see if it could be scaled in an emergency.

He had no expectation of an emergency, because he knew nothing of the law of the ledge. Having already met a doe and a bear, he naturally inferred that he would not be likely to meet any other of the elusive kindreds of the wild, even in a whole week of forest faring. The shy and wary beasts are not given to thrusting themselves upon man's dangerous notice, and it was hard enough to find them, with all his woodcraft, even when he was out to look for them. He was, therefore, so surprised that he could hardly believe his eyes when, on rounding another corrugation of the rock-face, he saw another bear coming to meet him.

"Gee!" muttered Peddler to himself. "Who's been lettin' loose the menagerie? Or hev I got the nightmare, mebbe?"

The bear was about fifty yards distant--a smaller one than its predecessor, and much younger also, as was obvious to Peddler's initiated eye by the trim glossiness of its coat. It halted the instant it caught sight of Peddler. But Peddler, for his part, kept right on, without showing the least sign of hesitation or surprise. This bear, surely, would give way before him. The beast hesitated, however. It was manifestly afraid of the man. It backed a few paces, whimpering in a worried fashion, then stopped, staring up the rock-wall above it, as if seeking escape in that impossible direction.

"If ye're so skeered o' me as ye look," demanded Peddler, in a crisp voice, "why in h--ll don't ye turn an' vamoose, 'stead o' backin' an' fillin' that way? Ye can't git up that there rock, 'less ye're a fly."

The ledge at that point was a comparatively wide and easy path; and the bear at length, as if decided by the easy confidence of Peddler's tones, turned and retreated. But it went off with such reluctance, whimpering anxiously the while, that Peddler was forced to the conclusion there must be something coming up the trail which it was dreading to meet. At this idea Peddler was delighted, and hurried on as closely as possible at the retreating animal's heels. The bear, he reflected, would serve him as an excellent advance guard, protecting him perfectly from surprise, and perhaps, if necessary, clearing the way for him. He chuckled to himself as he realised the situation, and the bear, catching the incomprehensible sound, glanced nervously over its shoulder and hastened its retreat as well as the difficulties of the path would allow.

The trail was now descending rapidly, though irregularly, towards the eastern plateau. The descent was broken by here and there a stretch of comparatively level going, here and there a sharp though brief rise, and at one point the ledge was cut across by a crevice some four feet in width. As a jump, of course, it was nothing to Peddler; but in spite of himself he took it with some trepidation, for the chasm looked infinitely deep, and the footing on the other side narrow and precarious. The bear, however, had seemed to take it quite carelessly, almost in its stride, and Peddler, not to be outdone, assumed a similar indifference.

It was not long, however, before the enigma of the bear's reluctance to retrace its steps was solved. The bear, with Peddler some forty or fifty paces behind, was approaching one of those short steep rises which broke the general descent. From the other side of the rise came a series of heavy breathings and windy grunts.

"Moose, by gum!" exclaimed Peddler. "Now, I'd like to know if all the critters hev took it into their heads to cross Old Bald Face to-day!"

The bear heard the gruntlings also, and halted unhappily, glancing back at Peddler.

"Git on with it!" ordered Peddler sharply. And the bear, dreading man more than moose, got on.

The next moment a long, dark, ominous head, with massive, overhanging lip and small angry eyes, appeared over the rise. Behind this formidable head laboured up the mighty humped shoulders and then the whole towering form of a moose-bull. Close behind him followed two young cows and a yearling calf.

"Huh! I guess there's goin' to be some row!" muttered Peddler, and cast his eyes up the rock-face, to look for a point of refuge in case his champion should get the worst of it.

At sight of the bear the two cows and the yearling halted, and stood staring, with big ears thrust forward anxiously, at the foe that barred their path. But the arrogant old bull kept straight on, though slowly, and with the wariness of the practised duellist. At this season of the year his forehead wore no antlers, indeed, but in his great knife-edged fore-hooves he possessed terrible weapons which he could wield with deadly dexterity. Marking the confidence of his advance, Peddler grew solicitous for his own champion, and stood motionless, dreading to distract the bear's attention.

But the bear, though frankly afraid to face man, whom he did not understand, had no such misgivings in regard to moose. He knew how to fight moose, and he had made more than one good meal, in his day, on moose calf. He was game for the encounter. Reassured to see that the man was not coming any nearer, and possibly even sensing instinctively that the man was on his side in this matter, he crouched close against the rock and waited, with one huge paw upraised, like a boxer on guard, for the advancing bull to attack.

He had not long to wait.

The bull drew near very slowly, and with his head held high as if intending to ignore his opponent. Peddler, watching intently, felt some surprise at this attitude, even though he knew that the deadliest weapon of a moose was its fore-hooves. He was wondering, indeed, if the majestic beast expected to press past the bear without a battle, and if the bear, on his part, would consent to this highly reasonable arrangement. Then like a flash, without the slightest warning, the bull whipped up one great hoof to the height of his shoulder and struck at his crouching adversary.

The blow was lightning swift, and with such power behind it that, had it reached its mark, it would have settled the whole matter then and there. But the bear's parry was equally swift. His mighty forearm fended the stroke so that it hissed down harmlessly past his head and clattered on the stone floor of the trail. At the same instant, before the bull could recover himself for another such pile-driving blow, the bear, who had been gathered up like a coiled spring, elongated his body with all the force of his gigantic hindquarters, thrusting himself irresistibly between his adversary and the face of the rock, and heaving outwards.

These were tactics for which the great bull had no precedent in all his previous battles. He was thrown off his balance and shouldered clean over the brink. By a terrific effort he turned, captured a footing upon the edge with his fore-hooves, and struggled frantically to drag himself up again upon the ledge. But the bear's paw struck him a crashing buffet straight between the wildly staring eyes. He fell backwards, turning clean over, and went bouncing, in tremendous sprawling curves, down into the abyss.

Upon the defeat of their leader the two cows and the calf turned instantly--which the ledge at this point was wide enough to permit--and fled back down the trail at a pace which seemed to threaten their own destruction. The bear followed more prudently, with no apparent thought of trying to overtake them. And Peddler kept on behind him, taking care, however, after this exhibition of his champion's powers, not to press him too closely.

The fleeing herd soon disappeared from view. It seemed to have effectually cleared the trail before it, for the curious procession of the bear and Peddler encountered no further obstacles.

After about an hour the lower slopes of the mountain were reached. The ledge widened and presently broke up, with trails leading off here and there among the foothills. At the first of these that appeared to offer concealment the bear turned aside and vanished into a dense grove of spruce with a haste which seemed to Peddler highly amusing in a beast of such capacity and courage. He was content, however, to be so easily quit of his dangerous advance guard.

"A durn good thing for me," he mused, "that that there b'ar never got up the nerve to call my bluff, or I might 'a' been layin' now where that unlucky old bull-moose is layin', with a lot o' flies crawlin' over me."

And as he trudged along the now easy and ordinary trail, he registered two discreet resolutions--first, that never again would he cross Old Bald Face without his gun and his axe; and second, that never again would he cross Old Bald Face at all, unless he jolly well had to.

The Morning of the Silver Frost

All night the big buck rabbit--he was really a hare, but the backwoodsman called him a rabbit--had been squatting on his form under the dense branches of a young fir tree. The branches grew so low that their tips touched the snow all round him, giving him almost perfect shelter from the drift of the storm. The storm was one of icy rain, which everywhere froze instantly as it fell. All night it had been busy encasing the whole wilderness--every tree and bush and stump, and the snow in every open meadow or patch of forest glade--in an armour of ice, thick and hard and glassy clear. And the rabbit, crouching motionless, save for an occasional forward thrust of his long, sensitive ears, had slept in unwonted security, knowing that none of his night-prowling foes would venture forth from their lairs on such a night.

At dawn the rain stopped. The cold deepened to a still intensity. The clouds lifted along the eastern horizon, and a thin, icy flood of saffron and palest rose washed down across the glittering desolation. The wilderness was ablaze on the instant with elusive tongues and points of coloured light--jewelled flames, not of fire, but of frost. The world had become a palace of crystal and opal, a dream-palace that would vanish at a touch, a breath. And, indeed, had a wind arisen then to breathe upon it roughly, the immeasurable crystal would have shattered as swiftly as a dream, the too-rigid twigs and branches would have snapped and clattered down in ruin.

The rabbit came out from under his little ice-clad fir tree, and, for all his caution, the brittle twigs broke about him as he emerged, and tinkled round him sharply. The thin, light sound was so loud upon the stillness that he gave a startled leap into the air, landing many feet away from his refuge. He slipped and sprawled, recovered his foothold, and stood quivering, his great, prominent eyes trying to look in every direction at once, his ears questioning anxiously to and fro, his nostrils twitching for any hint of danger.

There was no sight, sound, or scent, however, to justify his alarm, and in a few seconds, growing bolder, he remembered that he was hungry. Close by he noticed the tips of a little birch sapling sticking up above the snow. These birch-tips, in winter, were his favourite food. He hopped toward them, going circumspectly over the slippery surface, and sat up on his hindquarters to nibble at them. To his intense surprise and disappointment, each twig and aromatic bud was sealed away, inaccessible, though clearly visible, under a quarter inch of ice. Twig after twig he investigated with his inquiring, sensitive cleft nostrils, which met everywhere the same chill reception. Round and round the tantalising branch he hopped, unable to make out the situation. At last, thoroughly disgusted, he turned his back on the treacherous birch bush and made for another, some fifty yards down the glade.

As he reached it he stopped short, suddenly rigid, his head half turned over his shoulder, every muscle gathered like a spring wound up to extreme tension. His bulging eyes had caught a movement somewhere behind him, beyond the clump of twigs which he had just left. Only for a second did he remain thus rigid. Then the spring was loosed. With a frantic bound he went over and through the top of the bush. The shattered and scattered crystals rang sharply on the shining snow-crust. And he sped away in panic terror among the silent trees.

From behind the glassy twigs emerged another form, snow-white like the fleeting rabbit, and fled in pursuit--not so swiftly, indeed, as the rabbit--with an air of implacable purpose that made the quarry seem already doomed. The pursuer was much smaller than his intended victim, very low on the legs, long-bodied, slender, and sinuous, and he moved as if all compacted of whipcord muscle. The grace of his long, deliberate bounds was indescribable. His head was triangular in shape, the ears small and close-set, the black-tipped muzzle sharply pointed, with the thin, black lips upcurled to show the white fangs as if in a ferocious but soundless snarl, and the eyes glowed red with blood-lust. Small as it was, there was something terrible about the tiny beast, and its pursuit seemed as inevitable as Fate. At each bound its steel-hard claws scratched sharply on the crystal casing of the snow, and here and there an icicle from a snapped twig went ringing silverly across the gleaming surface.

For perhaps fifty yards the weasel followed straight upon the rabbit's track. Then he swerved to the right. He had lost sight of his quarry. But he knew its habits in flight. He knew it would run in a circle, and he took a chord of that circle, so as to head the fugitive off. He knew he might have to repeat this manoeuvre several times, but he had no doubts as to the result. In a second or two he also had disappeared among the azure shadows and pink-and-saffron gleams of the ice-clad forest.

For several minutes the glade was empty, still as death, with the bitter but delicate glories of the winter dawn flooding ever more radiantly across it. On a sudden the rabbit appeared again, this time at the opposite side of the glade. He was running irresolutely now, with little aimless leaps to this side and to that, and his leaps were short and lifeless, as if his nerve-power were getting paralysed. About the middle of the glade he seemed to give up altogether, as if conquered by sheer panic. He stopped, hesitated, wheeled round, and crouched flat upon the naked snow, trembling violently, and staring, with eyes that started from his head, at the point in the woods which he had just emerged from.

A second later the grim pursuer appeared. He saw his victim awaiting him, but he did not hurry his pace by a hair's-breadth. With the same terrible deliberation he approached. Only his jaws opened, his long fangs glistened bare; a blood-red globule of light glowed redder at the back of his eyes.

One more of those inexorable bounds, and he would have been at his victim's throat. The rabbit screamed.

At that instant, with a hissing sound, a dark shadow dropped out of the air. It struck the rabbit. He was enveloped in a dreadful flapping of wings. Iron talons, that clutched and bit like the jaws of a trap, seized him by the back. He felt himself partly lifted from the snow. He screamed again. But now he struggled convulsively, no longer submissive to his doom, the hypnotic spell cast upon him by the weasel being broken by the shock of the great hawk's unexpected attack.

But the weasel was not of the stuff or temper to let his prey be snatched thus from his jaws. Cruel and wanton assassin though he was, ever rejoicing to kill for the lust of killing, long after his hunger was satisfied, he had the courage of a wounded buffalo. A mere darting sliver of white, he sprang straight into the blinding confusion of those great wings.

He secured a hold just under one wing, where the armour of feathers was thinnest, and began to gnaw inwards with his keen fangs. With a startled cry, the hawk freed her talons from the rabbit's back and clutched frantically at her assailant. The rabbit, writhing out from under the struggle, went leaping off into cover, bleeding copiously, but carrying no fatal hurt. He had recovered his wits, and had no idle curiosity as to how the battle between his enemies would turn out.

The hawk, for all her great strength and the crushing superiority of her weapons, had a serious disadvantage of position. The weasel, maintaining his deadly grip and working inwards like a bull-dog, had hunched up his lithe little body so that she could not reach it with her talons. She tore furiously at his back with her rending beak, but the amazingly tough, rubbery muscles resisted even that weapon to a certain degree. At last, securing a grip with her beak upon her adversary's thigh, she managed to pull the curled-up body out almost straight, and so secured a grip upon it with one set of talons.

That grip was crushing, irresistible, but it was too far back to be immediately fatal. The weasel's lithe body lengthened out under the agonising stress of it, but it could not pull his jaws from their grip. They continued inexorably their task of gnawing inwards, ever inwards, seeking a vital spot.

The struggle went on in silence, as far as the voices of both combatants were concerned. But the beating of the hawk's wings resounded on the glassy-hard surface of the snow. As the struggle shifted ground, those flapping wings came suddenly in contact with a bush, whose iced twigs were brittle as glass and glittering like the prisms of a great crystal candelabra. There was a shrill crash and a thin, ringing clatter as the twigs shattered off and spun flying across the crust.

The sound carried far through the still, iridescent spaces of the wilderness. It reached the ears of a foraging fox, who was tip-toeing with dainty care over the slippering crust. He turned hopefully to investigate, trusting to get a needed breakfast out of some fellow-marauder's difficulties. At the edge of the glade he paused, peering through a bush of crystal fire to size up the situation before committing himself to the venture.

Desperately preoccupied though she was, the hawk's all-seeing eyes detected the red outlines of the fox through the bush. With a frantic beating of her wings she lifted herself from the snow. The fox darted upon her with a lightning rush and a shattering of icicles. He was just too late. The great bird was already in the air, carrying her deadly burden with her. The fox leapt straight upwards, hoping to pull her down, but his clashing jaws just failed to reach her talons. Labouring heavily in her flight, she made off, striving to gain a tree-top where she might perch and once more give her attention to the gnawing torment which clung beneath her wing.

The fox, being wise, and seeing that the hawk was in extremest straits, ran on beneath her as she flew, gazing upwards expectantly.

The weasel, meanwhile, with that deadly concentration of purpose which characterises his tribe, paid no heed to the fact that he was journeying through the air. And he knew nothing of what was going on below. His flaming eyes were buried in his foe's feathers, his jaws were steadily working inwards toward her vitals.

Just at the edge of the glade, immediately over the top of a branchy young paper-birch which shot a million coloured points of light in the sunrise, the end came. The fangs of the weasel met in the hawk's wildly throbbing heart. With a choking burst of scarlet blood it stopped.

Stone dead, the great marauder of the air crashed down through the slim birch-top, with a great scattering of gleams and crystals. With wide-sprawled wings she thudded down upon the snow-crust, almost under the fox's complacent jaws. The weasel's venomous head, covered with blood, emerged triumphant from the mass of feathers.

As the victor writhed free, the fox, pouncing upon him with a careless air, seized him by the neck, snapped it neatly, and tossed the long, limp body aside upon the snow. He had no use for the rank, stringy meat of the weasel when better fare was at hand. Then he drew the hawk close to the trunk of the young birch, and lay down to make a leisurely breakfast.

THE END

www.ingramcontent.com/pod-product-compliance
Lightning Source LLC
Chambersburg PA
CBHW071058290526
45795CB00004B/1559